KINGDOM
OF THE SUN

RUTH KAREN

KINGDOM
OF THE SUN

THE INCA:
EMPIRE BUILDERS OF THE AMERICAS

FOUR WINDS PRESS
NEW YORK

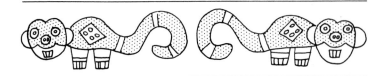

LIBRARY OF CONGRESS CATALOGING IN PUBLICATION DATA

Karen, Ruth.
  Kingdom of the sun.

  Includes index.
  SUMMARY: Discusses the culture of the Incas of
Peru including their customs, daily life, art, and
architecture.
  1. Incas. [1. Incas] I. Title.
F3429.K34   985   75–9886
ISBN 0–590–17288–3

Published by Four Winds Press
A Division of Scholastic Magazines, Inc., New York, N.Y.
Copyright © 1975 by Ruth Karen
All Rights Reserved
Printed in the United States of America
Library of Congress Catalog Card Number: 75–9886
5   4   3   2   1   75   76   77   78   79

By the same author

THE LAND AND PEOPLE OF CENTRAL AMERICA

NEIGHBORS IN A NEW WORLD: THE ORGANIZATION OF AMERICAN STATES

THE SEVEN WORLDS OF PERU

HELLO GUATEMALA

SONG OF THE QUAIL: THE WONDROUS WORLD OF THE MAYA

CONTENTS

MAP *xii*

KINGDOM
OF THE SUN

CARIBBEAN SEA

N. ATLANTIC OCEAN

VENEZUELA

COLOMBIA

BRIT.
GUIANA

SURI
NAM FR. GUIANA

EQUATOR

QUITO

ECUADOR

P
E
R
U

BRAZIL

LIMA

LA PAZ
BOLIVIA

PACIFIC OCEAN

PARAGUAY

TROPIC OF CAPRICORN

C
H
I
L
E

TUCUMÁN

URUGUAY

SANTIAGO

ARGENTINA

S. ATLANTIC OCEAN

SOUTH AMERICA

Legend

PERU

The Inca Empire at Its Zenith

N

W   E

S

Maps by Lucy Martin Bitzer

The Inca Empire at Its Zenith

Legend

MODERN CITIES ◉ ●
ARCHAEOLOGICAL SITES ▲
HIGHLANDS
MOUNTAINS

0   50   100 MILES
SCALE

COLOMBIA

EQUATOR

QUITO ◉

ECUADOR

GUAYAQUIL ●

IQUITOS ●

Amazon

PERU

Marañón

Vicus ▲

Piura ●

Lambayeque ▲

CAJAMARCA ●

TRUJILLO ●
Chan Chan ▲

Huallaga

Ucayali

BRAZIL

✳ MT. HUASCARÁN
Chavín de Huantar ▲

Chancay ▲

Rímac

LIMA ◉
Pachacamac ●

Curayacu ▲

Apurímac

Wari ▲

Machu Picchu ▲
Ollantaytambo ▲

CUZCO ●

Paracas ▲

Nazca ▲

BOLIVIA

Lake Titicaca

AREQUIPA ●

LA PAZ ◉
Tiahuanaco ▲

PACIFIC OCEAN

N

PART ONE

Close to the roof of the Americas, the ruins of Machu Picchu.
NOEL WERRETT

I THE REFUGE
THAT
TOUCHES
THE STARS

 Close to the roof of the Americas, clinging to a broad ledge of rock, huddle the ruins of Machu Picchu. The massive blocks of stone which remain of the palaces and temples that once ruled this summit, look precarious against the two thousand-foot ravine plummeting to a river gorge on one side, and the chain of Andean peaks on the other. The craggy profiles of these mountains dwarf anything beneath them. The peaks are above the treeline and therefore empty of vegetation. They are stark brown in the summer, glistening white in the winter. The air is thin at altitudes of three miles and more, and the sun, halfway between the equator and the Tropic of Capricorn, is close. In this light and air, Machu Picchu can seem like a mirage.

It *was* a mirage to the Spanish conquerors of South America who long hunted for this hidden Indian fortress and never found it. To the men and women who spent their lives in its remote fastness it was a refuge, a refuge that touched the stars and recalled their origins and their glory. The residents of Machu Picchu were the last of the Incas, a small highland tribe that became an imperial court and caste and, for about a century, ruled most of what was known of the South American continent until the Spaniards came.

In the Americas, the Inca empire was comparable to that of the Romans in ancient Europe—in size, cohesion and impact. And it was superior to Rome in the safety it offered its subjects. The Romans brought law and order. The Incas supplied security from the cradle to the grave; they constructed the most complete welfare state mankind has known.

In Machu Picchu you can see impressive fragments of this power. You can saunter through long, low stone dwellings or high, round stone tombs, past the mysterious "House of the Chosen Women" to the plaza at the top of the city, where "the hitching post of the sun" casts its stark and meaningful shadow. You can stop in a public square five centuries old and look around at steep mountainsides that have been carefully terraced to grow crops, with irrigation canals running through them still, and evidence that half a millennium ago the Inca knew enough about every aspect of agricultural production to feed a royal court and its large entourage from the harvest they wrested off these barren highlands. You can look down on the fountains and baths that dot this imperial summit city; peer through the elegantly shaped trapezoid windows to see a piece of road, built five centuries ago, straight as an arrow, or gaze into the black-green gorge that was arched by a suspension

*Stone dwellings and terraces in Machu Picchu, and the
central plaza with "the hitching post of the sun."*
COURTESY OF THE AMERICAN MUSEUM OF NATURAL HISTORY

Amid the towering crags of the Andes, the Inca built
their solid stone structures.
NOEL WERRETT

bridge of twisted fiber and woven ossier, swinging across the gorge like a giant hammock.

And you cannot help but wonder: Why did this social structure so solid in appearance crash and crumble so very quickly when it met up with the Spaniards in 1532–33? What price did the Incas and their subjects pay for their once glorious Kingdom of the Sun? And do the Inca ghosts hovering over these rock-ribbed valleys perhaps have a message for us today?

This much we do know about the Inca civilization:

At its zenith, the Inca empire was a marvel of organized diversity, with each individual fitted into a social web so thoughtfully and intricately made that it appeared silken and seamless.

At that time, the Inca empire encompassed all of what today is Peru; large parts of Chile, Bolivia and Ecuador; and sections of Argentina and Paraguay. It reached to the tawny coast of the Pacific, much of it arid sand dunes interspersed with fertile valleys, nature-made by rivers or man-made by irrigation in the south, and turning in the north into the luxurious verdancy of the equatorial belt. It covered the temperate plateaus and naked tips of the Andes, the highest of them piercing the clouds at more than twenty thousand feet. It encompassed the lush trans-Andean hills and lowlands, dipping and finally losing themselves in the jungles of Amazonia. The Incas governed all of these widely varied lands with finely calculated equity and an administrative machinery so superbly effective that it succeeded in welding the disparate peoples and civilizations that had grown, flourished and, in some instances, already decayed in these lands, into a single interdependent unit: a family of nations.

There were good reasons why almost anyone living in the Americas at that time would have wanted to belong to that far-flung family. In an age when everywhere else in the world most men and women had cause to fear hunger, exposure, need in childhood and neglect in old age, the Kingdom of the Sun vouchsafed its subjects total security: physical, emotional and spiritual.

Physically, every subject of the Inca could count on enough food and drink to sustain him, whatever the success or failure of his own labors; on adequate shelter, matched to the requirements of the climate in which he lived; on clothes to suit his station in life on all occasions; and on the best of medical care available at the time.

Emotionally, every Inca subject was cozily fitted into a family group that spanned three generations, with each generation assigned its specific tasks and roles, supporting and sustaining each other.

The family group in turn nestled in a community—a village or neighborhood—to which it contributed its strength and abilities and on which it could count for support in all emergencies as well as in the ordinary course of life.

The community was wedged into a social pyramid as tightly fitted and smoothly finished as the stones in the palace walls of Machu Picchu. At the apex of it all glowed the reassuring warmth and glory of the ruling Inca, who claimed direct descent from the sun.

That claim had important practical meaning for the Incas. It meant that, through the good offices of their ruler, they could count on the sun rising again, to warm them and their flocks of llamas and to nurse their crops from seed to harvest. The ruling Inca caste knew enough about astronomy to be able to fix the seasons, and the Inca priesthood used that knowledge to convince the people of the clergy's powers of prophecy. The useful forecasts the priests made of solstice and equinox caused the people to feel that with the help of their Inca and the clergy they were protected against the unpredictable elements and securely tied to the heavenly bodies that played such a vital role in their lives. This gave them spiritual peace.

This triple-tiered security—physical, emotional and spiritual—was made possible by two basic social skills that have sustained all successful empires before and since: expertise and organization.

In the Inca empire, the expertise was focused on agriculture, which was as important to life and power in that age as industry is in ours. The Inca knew all there was to know about the growing of crops, using irrigation and fertilizer, and adapting the mode of agriculture to the terrain, the crop to the climate. Equally important, they had devised a system of distribution that made certain no subject of the Inca—from the simplest *puric* behind his hand-plough to the remotest princely vassal recently welcomed into the Inca fold—ever went without the requirements deemed appropriate to his station.

Throughout the empire, every resource—fields, flocks, fish, game, minerals or manufactured products—was divided into three parts. One part went to the producer for himself and the sustenance of his family and community. A second part was set aside for the "sun," which meant the priesthood and all ritual and ceremonial purposes. The third part was allocated to the Inca. This included not only the ruler and his family but all segments of society that worked directly for the state such as the military, educators, court attendants of a wide range and variety, and craftsmen. However lavishly the reigning Inca might choose to live and supply his court and his military and civilian dependents, he could not possibly consume this third share of the empire's output.

What the Inca did not consume was stored in a network of warehouses that covered the realm. If any part of the empire needed supplies because the harvest had been bad; because too many of its producers had been called to the army or enlisted in other forms of imperial service; because a natural calamity such as flood, drought, tempest or earthquake had plagued it; or even because it had not yet learned to apply Inca systems and techniques, this chain of warehouses was opened to meet the need.

Guaranteeing delivery not only *where* it was needed but *when* it was needed was a system of roads that threaded the empire throughout its length with two major highways, one in the highlands and one on the coast, and innumerable crossways running from the highlands west and east, joining coast and jungle. The roads were serviced by squads of messengers, permanently posted at regular intervals, the intervals calculated to cover a distance corresponding exactly to the space a young man in top physical condition could cover at his best speed.

Accounts of the warehouse contents were kept with the help of the Incas' famous *quipu*, a kind of abacus on strings that the messengers could easily carry at full run. The messengers reported who needed what, and what was available to meet the need. Delivery, mainly by llama and litter, followed in short order.

This system of social welfare, unique in its time and in some

*In Inca architecture, stones were closely fitted without
mortar and windows had a typically trapezoid shape.*
COURTESY OF THE AMERICAN MUSEUM OF
NATURAL HISTORY

ways unparalleled still, secured for the Inca's subjects freedom from want. Organization, incorporated in the army and the law, furnished freedom from fear.

The Inca army was so well designed, disciplined and, most important and rare for its day, supplied, that Inca subjects, including newly conquered ones, vied to serve in it. It was a beautifully functioning military machine. Anyone attempting to hold out against it was overwhelmed by its juggernaut efficiency. When the Inca empire was nearing the height of its influence, its military repute was such that its army rarely had to fight. In most cases, some clamorous sabre-rattling—or, more accurately, club and *bola* clattering—was enough to frighten foes into submitting to the Incas' wishes.

At that stage in their power, the Inca for their part wisely preferred diplomacy to force. Conquest in this period began with the Inca sending a high-ranking dignitary to the people he desired to absorb, to explain how much better off they would be if they became an integral part of the Kingdom of the Sun. Since this was frequently true, a fair amount of Inca empire building was completed in this fashion.

When the tactic did not work, the Incas resorted to psychological warfare. They assembled an army and moved it in the direction of the district they wanted to acquire. Only when this display of the flag did not produce the desired results either, did the Incas actually send their army into battle.

The method at this stage was to apply the full power of military might as briefly as possible. The moment an enemy surrendered, the army was called to a halt. There was no mop-up operation, no

*Machu Picchu's famous "hitching post of the sun"
told the hours, the days, the seasons.*
COURTESY OF THE AMERICAN MUSEUM OF
NATURAL HISTORY

vengeance, no looting. Inca policy was to regard all subject people as part of the family as soon as they had pledged allegiance. This done, they were treated exactly like every other member of the Inca family: sternly but justly, faced with demands and offered rewards according to Inca order and law.

Law in the Inca realm was a subtle and sophisticated structure with punishment designed not only to fit the crime but to take into account the status of each subject and the responsibilities the individual was expected to shoulder. If, for example, a peasant was caught stealing, the punishment meted out to him, while quick, was light. The person really called to account was the official immediately responsible for the thief's conduct who had to explain why the man had felt the need to steal. Officialdom in the Inca realm was built on a decimal system, with the lowest official responsible for ten citizens, the administrative pyramid rising in geometric proportions. The higher the official, the more the law demanded of him.

As a result of this system of *noblesse oblige* and its enforcement, administration in the Kingdom of the Sun was almost totally devoid of corruption. The mark of status was responsibility: assigned, accepted, executed. The Inca himself set the example. Each ruling Inca, when he assumed the throne, and at regular intervals during his reign, personally inspected his realm. These journeys were not ceremonial visits to big cities or famous sites. Inspection tours could lead the Inca to obscure villages in the far corners of the empire: a collection of stone huts clinging to the side of an Andean crag; or a group of palm-thatched cottages in the jungle; or fishermen plying their trade in reed-boats on Lake Titicaca. On these inspection trips the Inca was carried in a covered litter, a platoon of men preceding him to sweep clean his path, another platoon following with trumpets, flutes and cymbals. But the Inca could— and did—step out of his litter at any time, and walk into a peasant's house; or stop to inquire of a woman cooking a meal, or a child minding its toy, whether they were being looked after properly by those responsible for their welfare.

Law and order thus embraced every member of the Kingdom of the Sun and every Inca subject was safely wrapped in security. One would have thought such a system would last forever.

In fact, fewer than two hundred audacious Spaniards shattered the golden realm of the Inca in just over a single year. They brought about, with little more than gallantry and guile, the collapse of an empire that exceeded Spain many times in size, military might, productive capacity and administrative competence. They did this by pitting against the Inca empire one vital ingredient it lacked: individual freedom, and the ingenuity and enterprise that spring from such freedom.

The conquistadors were cruel and greedy, medieval in the narrowness of their assumptions, arrogant and hypocritical in their attitudes and their conduct. But they were also that uniquely human phenomenon: individuals conscious of their desires and their abilities and willing to explore both. They were what the Incas—organized, orderly, obedient—were not. They were their own men.

II OUT
OF LAKE TITICACA

Sophisticated and powerful empires usually have an elaborate mythology and a complex history. Not the Incas. Inca legends were few, and unconcerned with the mystery of creation, the evolution of the universe, or the development of mankind. They were simple stories, with almost a fairy-tale quality. And Inca history, while dazzlingly dramatic, is succinct and very brief.

Once upon a time, the Incas were told, two handsome creatures, Manco Capac, the first Inca, and his sister-wife Mama Ocla, rose out of the waters of Lake Titicaca, sparkling in a diadem of Andean peaks, at the bidding of their father, the sun. The Sun-father gave to the pair a golden rod and instructed them to push that rod into the ground wherever they stopped to rest in wandering through the land. When they reached a place where the rod sank deep into the earth, they were to stop, settle, and found the Kingdom of the Sun.

The rod sank deep in the Cuzco Valley, one of the ribbons of green that embellish the Andean plateau in Ecuador, Peru and Bolivia. Historically, Cuzco was the Incas' first known settlement and remained their capital as they grew from tribe to empire. They called it Cuzco, which means "the navel of the world."

As Inca power grew, the simple legend of Manco Capac and Mama Ocla picked up political

The Inca's attire was not very different from that of his subjects.
COURTESY OF THE AMERICAN MUSEUM OF NATURAL HISTORY

overtones. We know exactly what Inca youngsters were taught about their illustrious ancestors during the final days of the empire. It has come down to us from a young member of the ruling family who was in Cuzco at the time of the Spanish conquest. He later married a Spanish lady and moved to Madrid, there to write his memoirs. In Spain he was known as Garcilaso de la Vega, "The Inca."

He reports that when he was seventeen and living in Cuzco, with the Spaniards already triumphant, he got to wondering just what had caused the rise and fall of his own people. He asked his uncle:

> Who was the first Inca? What was his name? From whom was he descended? How did he come to reign? With what men and what arms did he conquer this great empire? In other words, what is the source of our wealth, and of our great feats?

These were valid and vital concerns for a young Inca in that period of torment and turmoil and, Garcilaso says, "the Inca, my uncle, was delighted with my questions for he loved to talk about these things . . . And here is what he told me:

At one time, all the land you see about you was nothing but mountains and desolate cliffs. The people lived like wild beasts, with neither order nor religion, neither villages nor houses, neither fields nor clothing for they had no knowledge of either wood or cotton. Brought together haphazardly in groups of two and three, they lived in grottos and caves and, like wild game, fed upon grass and roots, wild fruit, and even the human flesh. They covered their nakedness with bark and leaves of trees, or with the skin of animals. Some even went unclothed. And as for women, they possessed none who were recognized as their very own.

Seeing the condition they were in, our father, the sun, was ashamed for them, and he decided to send one of his sons and one of his daughters from heaven to earth, in order that they might teach men to adore him and acknowledge him as their god; to obey his laws and precepts as every reasonable creature must do; to build houses and assemble together in villages; to till the soil, sow the seed, raise cattle and enjoy the fruits of their labors like human beings.

Our father, the sun, set his two children down at

&ভ KINGDOM OF THE SUN

a place eighty leagues from here, on Lake Titicaca, and he gave them a rod of gold, a little shorter than a man's arm and two fingers in thickness.

"Go where you will," he said to them, "and whenever you stop to eat or to sleep, plunge this rod into the earth. At the spot where, with one single thrust, it disappears entirely, there you must establish and hold your court. And the peoples whom you will have brought under your sway shall be maintained by you in a state of justice and reason, with piety, mercy and mildness."

Not content with passing on to his nephew this political interpretation of the legend, the uncle then added what must have been the essence of Inca imperial propaganda, the justification of Inca rule.

"To the entire world," added our father, the sun, "I give my light and my brilliance; I give men warmth when they are cold; I cause their fields to fructify and their flocks to multiply; each day that passes I go around all the world in order to have a better knowledge of men's needs and to satisfy these needs. Follow my example: Do unto all of them as a merciful father would do unto his well-beloved children; for I have sent you on earth for the good of men, that they might cease to live like wild animals. You shall be the kings and lords of all the peoples who accept our law and our rule."

One other legend exists concerning Inca ancestry. It is known as the Tale of the Shining Mantle. Its theme is power, all facets of power: getting it; holding it; justifying it.

The shining mantle story revolves around the second Inca ruler, Sinchi Roca. His mother, the legend asserts, was distressed by the misery, ignorance and bestiality of the highland people. She decided that something should be done about it, and that her son, Sinchi Roca, was the man to do it. She sewed him a mantle covered with spangles of gold and told him to hide in a cave on a hillside overlooking Cuzco, clad in this garment. He was to emerge from the cave, at a moment she had calculated carefully, and announce to the people she had assembled in the valley below that he was the son of the sun, sent by his "father" to rule over the land. The moment she chose for Sinchi Roca to emerge was when the sun's rays struck full force on his mantle. Bouncing off the golden discs, the light of the sun sparkled and glowed, creating a glittering halo around Sinchi Roca, which convinced the people marveling below that he was indeed what he claimed to be: the son of the sun, sent to rule over them.

While Sinchi Roca still belongs to the period of Inca legend, some historic facts dovetail with this story. A number of tribes living in the Andean highlands at that time—the twelfth century—were composed of scattered family groups, with no cohesion or continuity as a community. They banded together only in times of war, when they were attacked or themselves set out to fight. In such periods, they elected a leader for the duration of the war. That leader was called a *sinchi*. The Inca tribe, perhaps a little more advanced than its neighbors in agricultural skills and living habits, also had the inspiration to provide itself with a leader who would hold it together as a community on a continuous basis, in peace as well as war. The first such leader was Sinchi Roca.

Thereafter, myth shades into history, covering about two hundred years. There is general agreement among scholars that the entire chain of the Inca dynasty contained thirteen rulers, and that the first eight governed from the beginning of the thirteenth century to the middle of the fifteenth. History, concrete and verified, begins with the ninth Inca, Pachacuti Inca Yupanqui, who ruled from 1438 to 1471, and triumphantly launched the Inca people on their imperial sweep.

Historic Inca hegemony lasted less than a hundred years, but in that single century a tiny highland tribe turned itself into the most successful empire builders the Americas have known. When historians draw parallels to Pachacuti and his son Topa, they reach beyond Rome for their comparisons—to the Greeks' Philip and Alexander, or to Napoleon.

In the two hundred years of legendary history that stretch from that first tribal leader in the shining mantle, Sinchi Roca, to the great conqueror, Pachacuti, other members of the dynasty made their contributions to the Incas' spectacular rise. Some contributed ideas, others deeds. Some showed extraordinary bravery in battle, others ingenuity in political innovation. Looking back, one can see clearly how the mosaic was fitted together that finally dazzled the world as the Kingdom of the Sun.

The third Inca, Llonque Yupanqui, who succeeded Sinchi Roca, extended the idea of uninterrupted government by adding to the permanent ruler the beginnings of a civil service. He created *curacas*, a class of professional administrators who acquired and practiced governmental skills and passed them on systematically to their offspring. The Inca dynasty was hereditary, and the class and occupation of *curacas* was made hereditary as well, adding cohesion and competence to Inca organization.

It was this same Inca, evidently a man of executive genius, who initiated the practice of the personal inspection tour. The kings of Europe never thought of it, except as an occasional whim, and even modern republican chiefs of state tend to put their ears to the ground only at election time. Llonque Yupanqui, after testing the procedure himself, decided a personal inspection tour by the reigning Inca was a crucial part of administrative wisdom and should be institutionalized.

The fourth Inca, Mayta Capac, was an educational pioneer. He decided that the Inca and his sons should be systematically trained in both government and war. Later, this concept was expanded into a school system that included not only the ruling Inca family, but the sons of *curacas* and the princelings of rulers who had come under Inca sway.

Mayta Capac also implanted in Inca imperialism two traits that contributed greatly to its success and were astonishingly sophisticated for their time: religious tolerance, and the ability to perceive, appreciate and absorb the cultural achievements of other civilizations. Under Mayta Capac, the Incas conquered Tiahuanaco, the ceremonial center of another highland people that had flourished several centuries earlier. The people of Tiahuanaco were great architects and from them the Incas learned their building arts, particularly the construction of massive and enduring walls by fitting stones together without mortar so carefully that a knifeblade could not be inserted between them. Walls built this way had withstood

Tiahuanaco inspired the Incas' architecture.
ANN MCGOVERN

time in Tiahuanaco for hundreds of years. Inca walls, built the same way, have lasted even longer.

Mayta Capac demonstrated his religious tolerance by recognizing as men of wisdom the wizards, soothsayers and herbalists in whom the highland tribes had put their faith before the Incas introduced their worship of the sun. Later, when the Incas acquired subjects with more advanced religious systems, they followed the same practice. They never denied the divinities of other cultures. Instead, they brought a representative of each local deity to Cuzco, to be enshrined in the Inca pantheon with full honors. Native religious practice was permitted to continue throughout the realm, but was crowned with the additional worship of the Incas' own supreme deity, the sun, and, of course, its representative on earth, the ruling Inca, son of the sun.

During the reign of Mayta Capac, the Incas also achieved one of their astonishing engineering feats. They constructed the first suspension bridge. It was made of aloe fiber and crossed a highland canyon.

Mayta Capac's son, Capac Yupanqui, the fifth Inca, was significant for having become an Inca at all. He was not the oldest son and was chosen over the brother directly in line of succession because that brother was not considered good-looking enough to properly represent the dynasty of the sun.

Capac Yupanqui's imperial gaze was fixed west, on the Pacific coast, where a chain of cultural groups, some of them headed by princes, a few quite powerful and with substantial hegemonies of their own, seemed to him to be ready for the boon of absorption into the Kingdom of the Sun. Capac Yupanqui also wanted to make certain that these princes were absorbed before it occurred to them to unite in opposition. He tackled them one by one, some by persuasion, some by pressure, a few by military power. His great achievement in the military area was the truly difficult feat of preparing an army of highlanders, used to the cold, bracing air of the mountains, to fight successfully in the hot, enervating lowlands, on terrain unfamiliar to them and in a climate they found punishing. The contrast was greater than it had been for the Roman army, with its soldiers from the Appian Hills, languishing under the arid heat of the Judean desert. For the Romans, this searing change turned what they had expected to be a minor campaign into a war that dragged on for years. The Incas, under Capac Yupanqui, accomplished their first coastal conquests in a matter of weeks. When Yupanqui died, the Inca empire already encompassed some hundred and twenty thousand square miles.

Inca Roca took up where his father Yupanqui had left off. While

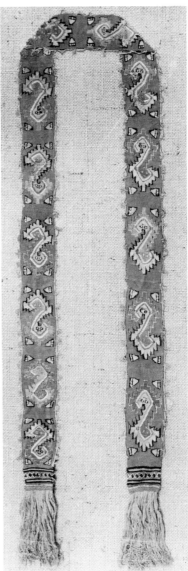

The Inca learned many of their skills from preceding civilizations. The coastal people were famous for their textiles and this tapestry belt, on a ground of rose-red wool, is the work of the Chimu. The tomb post, carved of wood, is typically Inca, but also comes from the coast.

his name was the same as that of the second member of the dynasty, this sixth Inca had come a long way from a tribal *sinchi*. He ruled an empire, which he aggrandized further.

Inca Roca extended coastal conquest south, to include the valley of the Nazca, a fascinating earlier civilization that was still vital and flourishing. Inca Roca also fought and finally defeated the Incas' main highland rivals, who by then had organized themselves into a political grouping of their own, the Chanca Confederacy. In pursuit of the Chanca, the Incas, for the first time, crossed the Andes in the east and incorporated into the empire trans-Andean hills and valleys—the *montaña*—where tropical crops were cultivated.

The *montaña* was the source of one crop, the pain-depressing stimulant *coca* (from which cocaine is derived), which has played an important role in Inca history. At the time of the empire, it was used for ritual purposes and to induce visions in the clergy and euphoria among the populace. During colonial times, it was employed as a stimulant to whip the Indians into exertion at work, particularly in the mines and on the large Spanish landholdings. In modern times, the descendents of the Incas, and the descendents of the people they conquered, reach for *coca* to alleviate the depression into which their dour and deprived lives thrust them.

Under Inca Roca, there was no need for pain relievers or anti-depressants. Inca Roca spent much of his energies bringing the pleasures of civilization to his realm. He beautified Cuzco, the capital; built the famous golden palace, *Cora Cora*, which the Spaniards encountered to their amazement and delight when they invaded Cuzco; and established the first *yachahuasi*, teachers' house, where a faculty of *amauta*, wise men, taught. It was the first

KINGDOM OF THE SUN

The Inca Roca brought many of the pleasures of civilization to his realm, including the products of other peoples. These jars and bowls were made by the Nazca and the Huari, both coastal people.

PHOTOGRAPH BY CHARLES UHT. COURTESY OF
THE MUSEUM OF PRIMITIVE ART, NEW YORK

formal school in the Inca empire, and the importance assigned to it by Inca Roca can be seen from the fact that he located the school on the palace grounds, right at the back of his own residence. While this was obviously a convenient location for the Inca princes who attended the school, it is quite possible that Inca Roca wanted it close so he could keep an eye on what was going on in this new institution he had devised and nurtured.

Another major Inca institution credited to Inca Roca played as important a part in the effective administration of the empire as did the education of the princes. This was the Incas' unique colonizing system, the *mitima*. When the Inca had absorbed a new people of whose loyalty they were not quite certain, they transferred some of the population to another part of the empire, importing in its place highland groups on whose loyalty they could depend. They were careful to organize such population transfers as humanely as possible, always in complete family groups and usually moving entire communities. They also tried to see to it that population groups that were moved ended up in a climate congenial to them and on land that had soil and weather conditions with which they were familiar. Such colonizers were considered the Inca's favorite children and were given special attention and care.

Garcilaso de la Vega, the Inca turned Spaniard, who reported his uncle's versions of the origin of his people, also describes and analyzes the *mitima* system.

"The Incas," says Garcilaso,

> transplanted Indians from one province to another for special reasons, some for the good of their vassals,

and others for their own purposes and to secure their
dominions from insurrections. In the course of their
conquests the Incas found some provinces to be naturally fertile, but thinly populated. To these districts
they sent Indians who were natives of other provinces
with a similar climate. This precaution was taken that
no injury might befall the settlers. On other occasions, when the inhabitants of a locality multiplied
rapidly, so that their province was not large enough
to hold them, they removed a certain proportion of
the people to some other district. They also removed
Indians from barren and sterile tracts to such as were
fertile and prolific, with a view to the benefit of those
that remained and of those that went; because, being
relations, they would help each other with their
harvests.

These productivity-minded population exchanges described by
Garcilaso were a later refinement of Inca imperialism. In the beginning the purpose was security, and Inca Roca was the first ruler
to move his loyal highlanders to some of the recently absorbed
territories on the coast.

Under Inca Roca's son, Yahuar Huacac, empire-building stopped
for a period. As the scholars put it, in succinct agreement: "Yahuar
Huacac didn't do much."

There may have been a personal reason. Yahuar Huacac's
mother, Mama Micay, was reputedly a very beautiful woman who
had been promised to the chief of the Aymara, a neighboring high-

land group, before Yahuar's father married her. The Aymara got angry at this and when Yahuar was about eight years old, they kidnapped him. The story is that the eight-year-old Inca was so outraged by this ploy that he wept tears of blood among his Aymara abductors. He was finally returned to his father, but the legend of his tears of blood came back with him, earning him the name Yahuar Huacac, which means "he who weeps blood."

He ascended the throne under that name, not an appellation particularly suited to inspire deeds of glory or feelings of safety among newly conquered subjects. Apparently Yahuar had enough sense to know that he was not an inspiring leader and that it would be best for him to stay put at Cuzco; this he did. His reign, however, is marked by an interesting personal act. He was the first of the Inca dynasty to reach out beyond the tribe for a marriage partner. The woman he married was an Aymara, a member of the clan that had abducted him and among whom he had shed his notorious tears of blood.

After the do-nothing reign of Yahuar Huacac, the political pendulum swung to the other extreme. Even the name of Yahuar's son was an indication of what was to come: the Kingdom of the Sun at its zenith; the beginning of a century of *Pax Incaica*. Yahuar's son, when he became the Inca, took the name of Viracocha, which means the Creator, in both the earthly and divine sense of the word. Perhaps Viracocha was trying to counteract the debilitating name that had bedeviled his father. Perhaps he was, as some Inca scholars think, "the first real Inca imperialist" planning not just to conquer or absorb other peoples but to weld them into a permanent political structure. And perhaps he felt that for

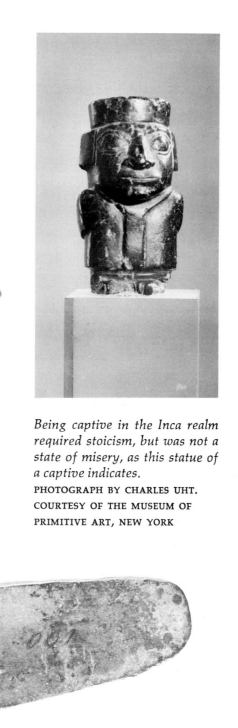

Being captive in the Inca realm required stoicism, but was not a state of misery, as this statue of a captive indicates.
PHOTOGRAPH BY CHARLES UHT.
COURTESY OF THE MUSEUM OF
PRIMITIVE ART, NEW YORK

An Inca knife, made of bronze. Such knives, finely honed, were used for surgery.
PHOTOGRAPH BY CHARLES UHT. COURTESY OF
THE MUSEUM OF PRIMITIVE ART, NEW YORK

political impact he needed a name of such all-encompassing appeal.

To an impressive extent, he lived up to his name. He consolidated Inca domain in the highlands, offering such honorable terms to his conquered neighbors that they became loyal vassals. He pushed the frontiers of empire southeast as far as what today is Tucuman in Argentina. And the reputation of his generosity as a conqueror and sagacity as a ruler was such that one powerful group in what today is Paraguay sent a delegation all the way across the Andes to request membership in the Inca empire.

The argument that delegation presented for its request was recorded by a Spaniard who in turn obtained it from an *amauta*, one of the teachers who, in their palace schools, passed on to their pupils a verbal and undoubtedly edited version of Inca history. According to the *amauta*, that delegation from the other side of the Andes said:

> Sapa Inca Viracocha. [*Sapa* is a title, meaning wise
> father.] The fame of the deeds of the Incas, your an-
> cestors, of the impartiality and rectitude of their jus-
> tice, of the excellence of their laws, of the care taken
> of their subjects, of their goodness, piety and kind-
> ness, and of the great wonders that your father, the
> sun, has lately worked through you have reached our
> land and passed beyond.

After this fawning introduction, which did, nevertheless, reflect quite accurately the reputation of the Inca empire by that time, the delegation noted that it was also interested in such practical and pleasurable fringe benefits as instruction in the Inca system of irrigation and land cultivation, Inca law, and, not least, the Incas' recipes for making their alcoholic beverage and their fine wool.

Some skeptical scholars suggest that this flattering delegation of volunteer vassals had more than technical assistance on its mind. What they really wanted was to deflect the Incas from extending their empire further east, and they did this by tipping off Viracocha to the interesting possibilities of expansion to the south and west in the direction of what today is Chile.

If this was indeed their motivation, they succeeded. Viracocha enlarged the empire to a total of about a hundred fifty thousand square miles, but his son and grandson, the Inca equivalents of the Greeks' Philip and Alexander, more than doubled that. They did it by incorporating not only the entire coast of today's Peru, including the kingdom of the Chimú, a powerful civilization in its own right, but also added to that the Pacific coast as far north as the Gulf of Guayaquil in Ecuador, and, in the south, half of today's Chile. In the south, they finally stopped at the Maule River, perhaps not entirely by choice. There they encountered the Araucanians, who resembled the Indians of the North American Plains in their desire to be left alone to live their own lives and follow their own ways. The Araucanians fought harder and more successfully than their counterparts in North America. The Incas finally gave up trying to subdue them, and the Spaniards never managed either. To this day, they exist as an independent group living in their own, largely traditional way.

Viracocha's son and grandson, Pachacuti Inca Yupanqui and Topa Inca Yupanqui, ninth and tenth in the Inca dynasty, are true historic figures. Their lives and achievements are known. No legendary aspects cling to them.

There are quotations and stories that illustrate the kind of men they were. From Pachacuti comes the dictum that conveys the essence of imperial conviction in its flat simplicity:

"When subjects, captains and *curacas* cordially obey the king, then the kingdom enjoys perfect peace and quiet."

Another Pachacuti maxim throws an interesting light on the psychological subtlety that accompanied this Inca's imperialism.

"He that envies another," observed Pachacuti, "injures himself."

Topa Inca displayed subtlety of a different sort. Pushing north to conquer most of what today is Ecuador, Topa Inca encountered a number of advanced cultural groups, with whom he worked out imperial arrangements quite easily. But he also came upon a group of fairly low cultural advance, who argued that they had no way to express their loyalty through tribute because they had nothing to give. Topa Inca, concurring with their claim to underdevelopment, instructed them to pay a tribute of lice.

By the time this unique imperial connection was established, the Inca empire was known as *Tahuantinsuyu* which means "the four quarters of the world."

The final territorial expansion of *Tahuantinsuyu* was achieved by the eleventh Inca, Topa's son, Huayna Capac. Huayna Capac planted the marker of the northern frontier, a row of boulders, at the Ancasmayo River, to this day the border between Ecuador and Colombia. At the time of Huayna Capac, these rocks delineated an empire of three hundred eighty thousand square miles.

Huayna Capac, Inca of the empire at its highpoint, also sowed the seeds for its precipitous fall. As in many European lands of the same period, it is the story of a dynasty undermined by personal passion and splintered by sibling rivalry.

Huayna Capac loved the northern country he had conquered, perhaps because it was lush and verdant, a sweet and comforting contrast to the barren, wind-swept highlands of his birth. He married the daughter of the king of the Quito, the dominant culture in Ecuador. They had a son whose fate it became to incorporate the final tragedy of Inca history.

His name was Atahuallpa and he started life happily enough as his father's favorite. But there were other sons, from previous marriages to Inca princesses, and the eldest of these, Huascar, was the legitimate heir to the empire. He was so proclaimed by the high priest in Cuzco after his father's death. Atahuallpa and Huascar never trusted each other, and their natural rivalry soon flared into armed conflict. For the first time since its legendary beginnings, the Inca dynasty failed to present a united front. There were rivalries within rivalries, splitting Inca families and the Incas' imperial structure. Most of the military apparently favored Atahuallpa, who was a talented warrior, while the clergy, hewing to tradition, generally supported Huascar. The dynastic rift also brought a collapse in the values that had built and sustained the empire. The half brothers practiced none of the generosity and sagacity with each other that the Incas had exercised so wisely and successfully with the peoples they had subdued. In their fraternal clashes, Huascar and Atahuallpa were ruthless and treacherous, cracking beyond repair the cement of civilization that had held together the Kingdom of the Sun.

III THE GREAT PRECURSORS

 An important part of Inca genius was its ability to assimilate what other cultures had to offer; to put to practical use in the empire the achievements of the peoples it conquered. The Romans had a comparable talent. But where the Romans were tolerant, the Incas were avid. The Romans, spreading out through Europe, Asia and Africa, appreciated accomplishments where they encountered them and accepted what pleased them, taking the process of absorption in stride. The Incas were sharper. They kept themselves deliberately alert to the excellencies of others, searched out other peoples' skills, and drank all this in with a hot intensity. This avidity for adaptation even led them to study the past of some of the civilizations they encountered, and they revived skills that had languished or lain dormant for centuries.

They had much to draw on. Many civilizations had come and gone in South America before the Incas emerged.

Since none of the South American civilizations had a written language, what we know about them is based largely on deduction

The Chavín were the earliest of the Incas' predecessors, and the feline motif decorating this bottle appeared in much of their art.
PHOTOGRAPH BY CHARLES UHT. COURTESY OF
THE MUSEUM OF PRIMITIVE ART, NEW YORK

from physical evidence: buildings and monuments, pottery, tools and ornaments, textiles, food, and skeletons.

Extrapolating from this evidence, anthropologists and archeologists name seven major periods in the history of South America.

The first is the Initial Period of the early farmers, when some of South America's seminal tribes turned from being itinerant nomads and hunters into settlers who cultivated crops. This period is put at 3000–1000 B.C.

Scientists call the next stretch of history the Cultist Period because in that time the first organized forms of worship appeared and spread. The greatest of the Cultist civilizations was that of the Chavín, who seem to have had a notion about man's evolution from the animal world, with the animal world symbolized by a feline creature resembling a jaguar.

The Cultist Period was followed by the Experimental Period, when civilizations experimented with political and social structures for about half a millennium. The Experimental Period extends to about A.D. 600.

With basic social structures formed, South America's civilizations turned to the improvement of life. Archeologists call this the Period of the Master Craftsmen, and the craftsmen of that era have left some splendid examples of their mastery. Theirs were the years A.D. 600–1000.

At that point, some of the South American civilizations started to look beyond their own borders. The scientists describe this development as the Expansionist Period. It lasted about two hundred years.

The Expansionist Period was followed by the centuries of the

City Builders, when the higher civilizations of South America evolved from aggregations of villages and ceremonial sites into political entities that were centered on cities: cities that contained the seat of government, were the focus of trade, and usually encompassed major religious edifices and the residences of the most important citizens. Enough remains of some of these cities to convey an idea of how large they were and, in some instances, how well planned. Chan-Chan, for example, the major city of the Chimú civilization on the Pacific coast, had meticulously plotted city blocks, designed as perfect squares, with about one block in every ten a garden. These gardens were situated at a level somewhat lower than the residential and commercial sections so that the people of Chan-Chan, walking along the streets, could look down and feast their eyes on the grasses and flowers that embellished their checkerboard city.

The period of the City Builders ended in 1450 (the Incas' own capital, Cuzco, was constructed during that time) and was followed by the flare of the Imperial Period, which historians bracket as the years 1450 to 1532. This was the age of the Incas.

The earliest precursors the Incas encountered were the Chavín in the highlands beyond the "white cordillera," so called because of the permanent snow of its peaks, which is the eastern chain of the Andes. The highpoint of Chavín civilization is generally given as somewhere between 800–500 B.C. The Chavín were very advanced for their time, technically as well as spiritually. They built three-story structures of stone—a feat that was not repeated in South America until two thousand years later. The corners of their buildings faced the four cardinal points of the compass, and the largest building, extant and now known as the *castillo*, the castle, contains perfectly functioning ventilator shafts.

You can see that Chavín "castle" yourself. It is situated in today's Peru, at a place called Chavín de Huántar, which is not easy to reach but well worth the effort. Enough is left of the *castillo* to provide an impression of the power and skill of these early Americans, contemporaries of the classic Greeks. In addition to the castle, one can contemplate *el lanzon*, the lance, a tall stone shaped much like a medieval knight's weapon. It is a monument of white granite, fifteen feet high, that seems to have served a religious purpose. It is elaborately carved, in a design of sophisticated lines and curves and, most significant, a stylized merging of the face of a man and a cat. Just what that humanized cat represented to the Chavín we do not know, but it seems to have had a religious meaning analogous to the cat of the ancient Egyptians. The Chavín's feline, however, looks less domesticated than that of the Egyptians, more as if it had been derived from a puma or a jaguar. Both these animals exist in the Andean highlands, and their power must have appeared awesome. Man in his earliest stages of evolution seems everywhere to have elevated his animal antagonists into deities, assigning to them the spiritual role that Christianity assigns to the devil. Thus contest and conquest assumed spiritual as well as physical meaning.

The most intricate manifestation of what went on in the minds of these very early Americans in the Andean highlands is a sculptured stone monument known as the *Raimondi Chavín*, after the man who discovered it, Antonio Raimondi. It shows the Chavín man-cat emerging and evolving, getting ever more abstract, until it climaxes in a crown of eyes and tails and what looks like a twisted rope ending in two serpents' heads, their tongues flicking.

The Raimondi Chavín, depicting the evolution of man.
PHOTOGRAPH BY CHARLES UHT. COURTESY OF
THE MUSEUM OF PRIMITIVE ART, NEW YORK

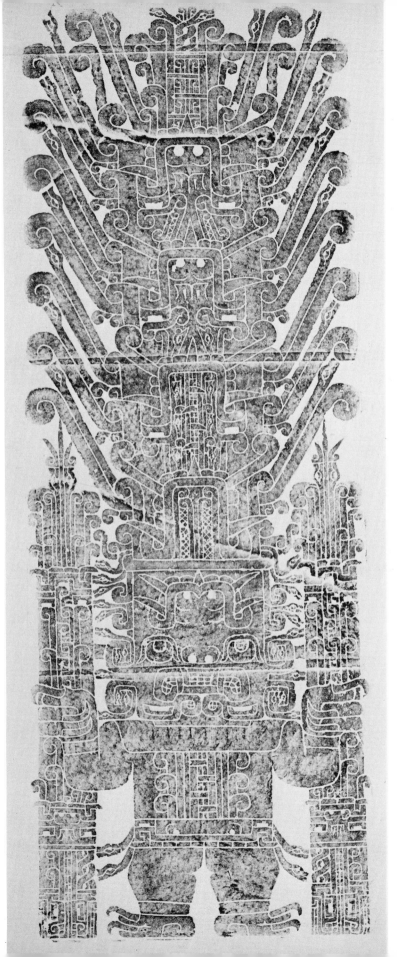

While we do not know just what the Chavín believed in, we do know that they spread their belief into the highlands north and south, and west across the *cordillera* to the coast, where the influence of their art can be seen to this day. Some anthropologists maintain that it was the greatest art style produced in South America.

What the Inca learned from the Chavín, however, had to do with a different kind of art: the art of human motivation and control, what today we would call social engineering. The Chavín experience taught the Inca that religious faith, and the practice of a cult, could constitute a unifying element in society, could be used to exercise political influence. The Inca designed their worship of the sun, and the rituals surrounding and sustaining that cult, for this political purpose.

For more down-to-earth, practical skills, the Inca delved into three important civilizations that started in the Experimental Period but properly belong in the time of the Master Craftsmen. In fact the period of the Master Craftsmen is named largely for the technical accomplishments of these three cultures, all of which developed along the rim of the Pacific, radiating from the coast of what today are northern, central, and southern Peru. The three civilizations were those of the Moche, the Paracas and the Nazca, with the Moche probably the earliest. The Moche left two major legacies to demonstrate their ability and give us a glimpse of what their life was like. The first illustrates the magnitudes of which Moche civilization was capable. It consists of two *huacas*—shrines —well preserved in the dry desert of northern Peru. Now called *huaca del sol*, the shrine of the sun, and *huaca de la luna*, shrine of the moon, they are pyramids of adobe brick squatting in the sand near the shore like giant turtles. The *huaca del sol* is the larger, with a base platform of 750 feet by 450 feet, and five terraces rising from the base. One scientist with a patient eye for detail has estimated the bricks in the structure and come up with a figure of a hundred and thirty million!

No arithmetic or scientific skill is needed to respond to the other major legacy of the Moche: their ceramics. In the form of vessels and bowls, jars and plates, these pottery utensils give an almost photographic rendering of persons and animals, human activities and habitats. Some Moche ceramics practically constitute a portrait gallery. To the Moche, ceramics were a representative art, and they produced portraits carved in clay the way painters in Europe produced portraits in oil. In addition to depicting specific individuals, these ceramics show doctors performing amputations, bone-setting or trepanning; warriors in battle dress; weavers at their looms; messengers on their way. They also show the animals the Moche knew: llamas and jaguars, frogs and dragonflies; the food the Moche ate; the boats they fished from; and the houses they lived in.

The Incas' most impressive practical achievements—agriculture and engineering—apparently owe a good deal to the Moche. The Moche built aqueducts for irrigation, some so good they are in use today. They also used fertilizer, called *guano*, the droppings of an offshore bird, which is so efficacious that the Peruvian government still maintains a monopoly over it. They also built roads which, while not nearly matching the famous Inca roads in length or durability, did tackle some of the geographic obstacles involved in the desert terrain of the coastlands and the steep inclines of the Andean

Mochica art was very realistic. This portrait is a jar.
PHOTOGRAPH BY CHARLES UHT. COURTESY OF
THE MUSEUM OF PRIMITIVE ART, NEW YORK

And this typical stirrup spout vessel is the portrait of
a woman.
PHOTOGRAPH BY CHARLES UHT. COURTESY OF
THE MUSEUM OF PRIMITIVE ART, NEW YORK

Mochica realism tells us a lot about the life of the Moche. These three effigies depict: a boy; a frog; a warrior.

foothills. The Moche also seem to have had an organized messenger service, which the Inca adopted and perfected. But Moche messengers were better equipped than their Inca successors in one respect. While the Moche had no written language either, they apparently had mastered the skill of inscribing a few memory-jogging ideograms on dried beans. Moche messengers carried these inscribed beans, in little bags, to their destinations. The Incas' *quipu* was a purely mathematical tool. The Moche's inscribed beans seem to have been able to convey ideas as well as numbers.

Finally, the Moche were fond of personal adornment. It was the men rather than the women who wore earrings, necklaces and bracelets, made primarily of metal. The Incas adopted all of these, showing a predilection for earrings. Inca earrings were often so large and heavy that they distended the lobe. When the Spaniards first encountered the Incas, the conquistadors were so struck by this fashion and its biological results that, among themselves, they referred to the Inca as *orejones*, big ears.

While the Moche were producing their great crafts in ceramics and metal, another civilization further south specialized in textiles. These were the Paracas, centered on a peninsula with soft waves of golden sand that seem to roll to the coast, there to merge harmoniously with the blue waters of the Pacific. The climate in the Paracas Peninsula is even, and very dry, which is fortunate because it made possible the preservation of the magnificent cloth that was the pride of the people of Paracas. The Paracas wove mantles, shirts, shawls, sashes and turbans, in brocade and lace, in double weaves and gauzes, using as their yarns the fine wool of the alpaca or varieties of cotton which they grew especially for the purpose.

The Paracas cultivated cotton plants that produced shades of fiber from the customary near-white, through eggshell and cream, to a brown almost as deep as cacao. The Paracas were also highly skilled at making and blending dyes to give them brilliant primary colors as well as a wide range of subtly shaded hues. They used the latter mainly for the exquisite embroidery with which they covered their garments in designs and patterns that combine variety with harmony, and inventiveness with order. The major Paracas garment was a floor-length mantle. The mantles of Paracas are classed with the finest handiwork of man.

The Incas were quick to adopt, and adapt, the skills the Paracas had developed in textile manufacture. But the Incas never reached the artistic heights of the Paracas. Inca garments, while sturdy for all, and finely woven for the ruling caste, were simple in cut and color. They had neither the magnificent flow of a Paracas mantle, nor the fine weaving techniques, nor the loving and expert composition of color and design. But from the Paracas the Incas did learn how to grow cotton for a variety of color and how to make cloth in a number of ways.

Not far from the Paracas, but a little later, flourished another coastal civilization that belongs in the period of the Master Craftsmen: the Nazca, who also made lovely textiles but poured their sense of color and harmony into highly polished, multicolored ceramics. Nazca vessels were too subtle for the Incas to copy, and perhaps also too luxuriant. The Incas were essentially an ascetic people, concerned with production and power, not luxury in any of its manifestations. And they considered the arts, major or minor, as luxuries.

48 ✑ *The Paracas excelled in textiles. Their mantles are world-famous. This sample illustrates why.*
COURTESY OF THE AMERICAN MUSEUM OF
NATURAL HISTORY

The Nazca poured their sense of color and harmony
into highly polished, multicolored ceramics like these
bottles and jar.

What the Incas did pick up from the Nazca was the Nazca's knowledge of the seasons, which seems to have been advanced for its time. There exists an intriguing mystery which suggests that the Nazca had a very special relationship with celestial bodies, scientific, spiritual, or both. In the land the Nazcas inhabitated lies a valley, about forty miles long and one mile wide. It is an area of pebbles, each pebble about the size of a fist, which millennia of sun and air have oxidized to a dark green-brown. Beneath, the ground is cream colored, a combination of sand and gravel. Sometime in the history of their civilization, the Nazca picked up these fist-sized pebbles in a carefully designed pattern, piling up the stones at the edge of the valley and leaving the light sand beneath exposed in lines and patterns. The patterns include a big bird in flight, a crab, and a composition of fluid lines and curlicues that looks like a bouquet of posies. Part of the intricate design consists of patterns running in the cardinal directions, and there are oblongs and squares that seem to delineate equinox and solstice in this region. The patterns can be comprehended only if seen from the air and the mystery they present is two-edged. How did the Nazca conceive designs that can be seen properly only from on high—and why? And just what do these designs signify? Anthropologists speculate that the pattern may have constituted a graph of the seasons, a kind of farmers' almanac. But who read it to the farmers?—and how?—and from where? All we can surmise is that the Nazca were apparently knowledgeable in matters astronomical, and that the Incas seem to have gleaned some of that knowledge.

We do know for certain, however, what the Incas learned from another highland civilization that preceded them, the Tiahuanaco, who rose to power in the area from which the first Inca, Manco Capac, reputedly came, thirteen-thousand-foot-high Lake Titicaca. The Tiahuanaco belong in the Expansionist Period. Their influence spread from the sky-piercing Andean highlands, some distance north of the Incas' Cuzco, across the two mountain chains and the valleys between them all the way to the coast.

A number of parallels exist between the Tiahuanaco and the Incas. Both were highland people, clearly concerned with power. Both were sufficiently organized to spread their power over a large distance. The Incas reached further than the Tiahuanaco, but the Tiahuanaco seem to have lasted longer. The guess is that their influence was felt for about four hundred years. It was, however, influence, not direct rule.

The Tiahuanaco also shared with the Incas a bent for austerity. Tiahuanaco art—as expressed in ceramics, textiles, metalwork and architecture—was simple and severe. It had neither the imaginative enchantment of the Paracas or the Nazca, nor the vivid realism of the Moche. Perhaps a penchant for austerity is a quality shared by highland people everywhere.

The Tiahuanaco and the Incas were almost neighbors, cousins of a kind. The Tiahuanaco were of Aymara stock, the same cultural group that abducted the seventh Inca, Yahuar Huacac, because his beautiful mother had originally been promised to an Aymara chief but had married an Inca instead. And there is a final parallel. In South America today, the only Indian languages still spoken widely are the Incas' language, Quechua, and the Aymara language of the Tiahuanaco.

The main accomplishment the Incas adopted from the Tiahua-

Inca buildings were constructed of massive stone blocks, and sometimes had lintels such as this one.
ANN MCGOVERN

naco was architecture. The Tiahuanaco were massive builders, who knew how to cut, move and fit stone, using insets, tenons and copper clamps. A Tiahuanaco sanctuary manifesting these skills still broods regally on a plateau near Lake Titicaca, on the Bolivian side of the lake. Its main feature is a massive gateway, carved of a single block of andesite rock, ten feet high and a little more than twelve feet wide. It is known as the "Gateway of the Sun," perhaps because the Tiahuanaco were already sun-worshipers themselves. Above the center of the doorway a face stares down sternly at the world. A god? A ruler? A ruler claiming to be a god? No one knows. But the Incas had an interpretation of their own. They thought that the central figure over the Gateway of the Sun repre-

A stone statue carved by the Tiahuanaco.
PHOTOGRAPH BY CHARLES UHT. COURTESY OF
THE MUSEUM OF PRIMITIVE ART, NEW YORK

A Tiahuanaco vessel with a puma spout.
PHOTOGRAPH BY CHARLES UHT. COURTESY OF
THE MUSEUM OF PRIMITIVE ART, NEW YORK

sented Viracocha, the original creator god who told Manco Capac
and Mama Ocla what to do. And the forty-eight smaller figures
carved on the same gateway, all of whom seem to be running toward that central, squared-off personage, are Viracocha's sketch
of the nations he was about to create. It is an imaginative notion.
Soaring ideas come easily in the rarefied air around Lake Titicaca,
where the sun really seems to be rising out of the lake at dawn, and
the mountains look as though they were whispering to the sky.

The latest of the great precursor civilizations with which the
Incas had contact was that of the Chimú who, at the highpoint of

their own power, ruled about six hundred miles of coastland, from present-day Lima to the border of Ecuador. For a period, the Chimú and the Incas were contemporaries. The Chimú had flourished earlier—their civilization is generally thought to have risen around the year A.D. 1000—and they finally submitted to the Incas in 1476.

The Chimú were resplendent representatives of the period of the City Builders, their capital, Chan-Chan, representing a model metropolis for its day. It was about eight miles square, laid out in regular blocks, with straight streets running along walled compounds of houses. Walls had sculpted friezes for decoration, regular bands of animals or humans, all surrounded by imaginative flourishes: flying fish, and diving men with streamers in their hair, and long-beaked birds that seem to be carrying weapons. The compounds were interspersed with sunken gardens, adding color to the mud-hue of the adobe structures, and an interesting skyline was provided by stepped pyramids that seem to have served religious purposes. Chan-Chan itself also has one giant compound, with deep niches in the walls, which seems to have been a seat of government where the ruler of Chan-Chan presided over political assemblies from his throne at one end of the compound, while the attending councilors, nobles and vassal chiefs parked their litters in the niches and spoke their piece from this position of relative comfort and privacy. How they were heard over such distances (the "government compound" in Chan-Chan is roughly the size of a modern city block) is hard to conceive. Perhaps they used messengers. The Chimú, like their predecessors on the coast, the Moche, had a messenger system. They also had roads, irrigation, and fertilizer. Their big step forward from the Moche, in addition to city building, seems to have been a system of political alliances concluded with the highland peoples to the east. The land the Chimú ruled is largely desert and they depended on the Andean foothills for their water. The alliances with the peoples of the east were made to protect that water supply.

The Chimú mass-produced their ceramics, using a mold, and their textiles and metal objects were mass-produced as well. They did some handsome work in silver and gold, of which they seem to have had an inordinate supply. Where they got the gold may well have been one of the secrets the Incas wrested from them, because the Incas, in their turn, astonished the Spaniards by the amount of gold they had amassed.

Chimú ceramics, though mass-produced, have a distinctive style that is quite beautiful. The most beautiful are finished in a high-gloss black that throws off a silver sheen reminiscent of the light of the moon over the ink-black Pacific as seen from the compounds of Chan-Chan.

The Incas did not copy the Chimú style—it was too rich and mysterious for their taste—but they did adopt the Chimú's mass-production techniques, the assembly lines of their day. It is also possible that the Incas learned from the Chimú's system of political consultation. As the Kingdom of the Sun expanded, and political problems became more numerous and complex, the ruling Incas worked out a system of consultation. All major decisions were made in council, a body, however, which consisted of Incas only. Its members had to be Incas by ethnic origin, as well as members of the royal family which, over the years, had grown numerous and become a caste.

IV AT HOME IN THE KINGDOM OF THE SUN

Caste played a vital role in Inca society. It served as the scrupulously drawn blueprint for the structure of empire. With very rare exceptions, every individual in the empire was born into a caste and stayed in it throughout life. Caste determined where a person lived, and how; it fixed occupation and decided marriage; it even indicated the clothes worn by man, woman and child, the food they ate, the beverage they drank.

The system enmeshed the individual from the moment of birth. It provided for twelve categories of persons, graded by age and sex.

For males, the first category was infants dependent on their parents, up to the age of one. During that year even the Incas did not expect a baby to make a contribution to society, but they did expect it not to interfere with its parents' productive activities. Infants were tightly swaddled and placed in a wooden box that served as a cradle. They were unwound from their cocoon only once a day, to be washed with cold water. Particularly loving mothers, an observant Spaniard reported, would warm the water in their own mouth before using it to clean up the baby.

*Up to age one, even Inca babies were dependent on
their parents.*
THE METROPOLITAN MUSEUM OF ART, GIFT OF
NATHAN CUMMINGS, 1964

There was no such thing as feeding on demand for the Inca infant. Babies were fed exactly three times a day, at exactly the same hours each day. All the howling in the world apparently made no difference, and presumably most babies gave up this first assertion of their personalities after a while. Babies were breast-fed for two years, then weaned.

From their second to their fifth year, youngsters belonged in a second category, that of "playing children." Once weaned, two holes were dug for them in the ground, one inside the house, another outside in the yard, and children were ensconced in one or the other of these pits, depending on the weather and the time of day. The holes were shallow enough for arms to stick out, but deep and narrow enough so the child could not climb out. They functioned as a kind of playpen, except that they contained no toys. Children were supposed to entertain themselves by watching adults at work or nature around them.

At age five they entered the third category, "children handling small tasks." This period lasted until they were nine and was, perhaps, the nicest part of an Inca's life. While in that category, boys helped their fathers with some of the easier chores, girls worked with their mothers the same way. But only part-time. There was time left for the children to play: with balls, tops and, for girls, rag dolls.

At nine, play came to an end and full-time work began. For boys this usually meant that they became shepherds, taking the llama herds to pasture, which was not always an easy task. Some of these pastures were narrow strips of grass wedged among mountain crags and the shepherd was responsible for getting each member of

When Inca boys turned nine, they often became
shepherds for flocks of alpacas and llamas, reproduced
here in silver.
COURTESY OF THE AMERICAN MUSEUM OF
NATURAL HISTORY

the flock there and back home without mishap. To this day, you can see in Peru Indian boys no more than ten years old looking after flocks in the Andean highlands. Under the Incas, the flocks consisted largely of llamas, occasionally alpacas and, rarely, a domesticated vicuña. Nowadays there are also sheep and goats, sometimes a cow or a horse. But the llamas are still the most important members of most flocks, and they look it. Their heads held high, they are frequently taller than their boy-shepherd and almost always look more sure of themselves.

Under the Inca system, the shepherd age ended at sixteen and was followed by categories five and six, encompassing respectively the years sixteen to twenty and twenty to twenty-five. These were the apprentice and journeymen periods during which young men became head shepherds, runners for their village governors, pages for officers on active service. The basic idea was for them to move about, widen their knowledge of their country and its people, learn what responsibility consists of, and how it is executed.

The following twenty-five years were dedicated to applying what they had learned. From age twenty-five to fifty, a man was slotted into the seventh category which, for most men, meant that they became the basic unit of the Inca system, a *puric*, the adult male who did the work of the kingdom. During that period, a man had to marry. He was given five years leeway to do this, but age thirty was the upper limit. He labored basically for his *ayllu*—his community—as a farmer, but was subject, along with every other *puric* in the empire, to being drafted for an array of public works: road construction, mining, service in the army, erection of public buildings, or any other service the ruling Inca might decree.

All these forms of public service were called *mita* and were considered a kind of tax. There was no tax evasion among the Incas, although some loopholes existed even then. Certain privileged tribes or communities were traditionally assigned specific services which they, and they alone, rendered and which exempted them from meeting any other form of *mita* obligation. Thus, the *purics* of the Rucan tribe were traditionally litter-bearers for the Inca and paid no other form of *mita*. The men from Chumpivilca were court dancers, and the Chicha carved firwood logs for ceremonial occasions.

The *mita* was levied annually, at the pleasure of the Inca, who decided what public services were needed, and what the contribution in manpower of each community had to be.

Every *puric's* basic task, however, was to cultivate the fields of his *ayllu*. All land was owned communally. Plot assignments were made each year with some land set aside to lie fallow for crop rotation. The remainder was divided up among the community's families, each allocation corresponding meticulously to the size of the family. The assigned family plot, however, was only one part of the land each *puric* had to work. His first obligation was to take care of the lands of the sun, that is, the lands that supplied the clergy, and the food and animals needed for ritual purposes. The *ayllu* worked these lands together, in teams.

Before the *puric* could get to his own family plot, he had yet another obligation: to help cultivate the lands that were set aside to feed widows, the disabled, and the "grass widows" of the men who were away on *mita* duty. This arrangement made it possible for the men paying their labor tax to do public service with an easy mind. They knew their families were taken care of in their absence, and that when they returned to their community they would find its lands in the same state in which they had left them.

Family plots were worked by the family alone, both men and women. If a family was large and consisted of energetic, hard-working members, this meant that they could, with effort, do just a little better with their land. Since the annual allocation of land was geared to family size, the difference could not be very great. There was, in fact, no way to get rich in the Kingdom of the Sun.

If a *puric* and his family, by dint of hard work, did accumulate a little more than they needed for their own consumption, in crops or animals, there was not very much they could do with it. The Inca empire had only the most marginal form of private trade. There was no currency. A market of sorts was held three times a month in every larger community, but trade in these markets consisted only of small-scale barter. A *puric* or his wife would crouch behind a little pile of whatever goods they had to offer and wait for someone to come by, proffering an exchange. The strange thing about these transactions was that they were completely silent. The trading was done mainly by gestures. Goods were weighed on scales, wordlessly.

In Peru today, some highland markets still follow the old patterns. Sellers sit behind their wares, spread out in piles on a mat or a cloth, and either nod, or shake their heads, as a buyer comes by with an offer. Modern Peru, of course, does have money, but in these highland markets trading is still quite frequently a matter of barter: a handful of red pepper for a small sack of powdered lime, a basket of potatoes for a pair of thonged sandals. No clink of money, and no words.

After working the plot of the sun and the land of the widows and disabled, the *puric* had a third field to look after: the field of the Inca. The products of that field went to the state, for use and for storage. Cultivating the Inca's plot was considered a privilege and pleasure. The men of the village set out in a team, dressed in their holiday clothes, with music to pipe them to the field, and the priest waiting for them to offer his blessing. Work on the Inca's field was begun each year with the governor of the community symbolically turning the first piece of sod. In Cuzco, the reigning Inca himself turned the first piece of ground each spring. He used a golden spade, a present, it was said, from his father, the sun.

Aside from having no choice in the matter—and not very much else to do—the *puric* perhaps did not mind working the fields of the Inca. He knew that, if there ever was a period of need in his own *ayllu*, the storehouses to which most of this product went would be opened for his needs. Working the Inca's fields was a kind of insurance premium.

The Inca system functioned smoothly because it deliberately designed and carefully promoted such labor-inducing motivations. To make certain, however, it also followed through with a supervisory mechanism that was pervasive. Each Inca personally inspected his realm, down to the tiniest facet. His example was followed at every level of administration. Supervisors stuck their noses into everything, including a man's home. Families, in fact, were encouraged to eat by the open door so that a supervisor could see at a glance whether the food was ample—but not too ample— clean and well prepared.

Men working in the fields were supervised at all times, and women were subjected to unannounced spot-checks in their homes. If a supervisor found a home dirty, he could order the slovenly housewife to eat the dirt in public. If he found food or beverages not clean enough, he could order the whole family to wash their faces, hands and hair in a bucket of water, then drink that same water—again in public. The idea, of course, was to teach the offending family better habits by holding them up to the ridicule of neighbors, warning the neighbors at the same time of what might happen to them if they should fall into bad habits. Checking into the cleanliness of a home included taking a look at the childrens' faces. No wonder parents stuck their children into cribs from which they could not move!

At age fifty a man entered the ranks of the semi-retired, category eight in the Inca schedule. From then on, he was exempt from all civic and military duties as well as from work on the land except in emergencies, such as harvest time. Men in that category became servants to the lower nobility, or to the Inca himself. Both were considered an honor. Some men were trained as *mayocs,* manipulators of the *quipu.* Others became *amautas,* teacher-historians. These men were instructed in Inca legends, which they memorized and recited to students in school or as entertainments at court functions and festivals. At that age it was also thought that men were sufficiently steeped in the Inca concept of public responsibility to be trusted with such positions as storekeepers, statisticians, and warehouse clerks.

At sixty, men entered the last of the categories for the average *puric,* retirement. The Incas called it the "eat-sleep" period, but it

Purics *spent their lives working the land, with implements resembling this ceremonial spade.* (Left)

Inca housing *was even simpler than this vessel-dwelling which comes from the coast.* (Right)

PHOTOGRAPHS BY CHARLES UHT. COURTESY OF
THE MUSEUM OF PRIMITIVE ART, NEW YORK

wasn't. The Incas did not believe in idle hands at any time. They said it made for bad thoughts. Men in category nine were assigned light tasks such as the twisting of rope for suspension bridges, the tending of domestic animals, and the "teaching of children." Teaching among the Incas at this level meant initiating a child into the Inca system of rewards and punishments. Since knowing this system, and learning to live within it, was vitally important in Inca society (disobedience could bring disastrous results not only for the individual but for his family and, in some cases, his entire *ayllu*), this role of the retired grandparents was treated with great respect. A Spaniard observing the family system at work, and reporting on the status of the old in Inca society, noted: "their experience of life was valued and their advice followed."

Three additional categories existed for males, for special cases. Into these belonged all invalids: the blind, the deaf, the handicapped. Such men married within their respective groups, were given a house and land, were not subject to the *mita* or other public service and, if they needed help to sustain themselves, that help was given by the community.

For women, life was laid out on a parallel route. The first two categories for girls were much the same as for boys. In the third category, at age five to nine, girls were given small tasks preparing them for their future labors. They would start to carry water and fodder, weed, spin and weave a little, help to make *chicha*, a corn beverage, and if there were infants in the house take a hand in the daily task of unswaddling and washing them.

Thereafter, the female categories spanned different ages than those of the males, as well as calling for different work.

For girls, category four covered the years nine to twelve. While the boys were out with the flocks, the girls would be out gathering herbs and flowers, not for decoration or savor—although some of the herbs were put to culinary uses—but for use as textile dyes, and for medicinal and ritual purposes.

The girls' fifth category started at twelve and finished at eighteen. This was the girls' counterpart to the boys' years of apprenticeship and was dedicated to familiarizing them with their life tasks: taking care of the home, making textiles, and, in some cases, learning the techniques of domestic service for use in the households of administrators or the nobility. Some girls became shepherdesses, a tradition that has continued in Peru to this day.

Category five also furnished the candidates—the most beautiful girls in the kingdom—for a very special career, that of "Chosen Women." Chosen Women became either "Virgins of the Sun," celibates dedicated to spiritual tasks and services, or wives and concubines for the ruling Inca, his far-flung family, and the minor nobility or military men and administrators whom the Inca wished to reward. Chosen Women were sent to a special training school at age twelve to be taught the higher skills reserved for women in the Inca division of labor: the weaving and embellishment of vicuña cloth, the preparation of delicate dishes, the concoction of special beverages, and the steps of sacred dances.

Women were considered adults at eighteen but their time as *purics*—the basic working category—ran for only twelve years, from eighteen to thirty. These were the child-bearing years, and Inca women had to be married by the time they were twenty. After thirty, women's lives did not change until their retirement at fifty, when they limited their activities to light household chores and the education of the young.

The Incas were not very romantic in the matter of marriage. To them it was simply another job to get done, another system to be enforced. Parents chose partners for their children, but could not move out of the *ayllu* to do so. This prevented tribal rivalries and cultural adjustment problems. Parents chose partners, but the government had to approve, and a public official performed the marriage. Every year, one day was set aside in each *ayllu* for a mass wedding. On that occasion, anyone who had reached the must-marry age but had not found a suitable partner was accommodated in revoltingly efficient fashion. All the boys of marriageable age were lined up on one side, the girls on the other. The governor of the *ayllu* walked down the line, decided who would pair well with whom, and married them right then and there.

Once married, a couple was assigned a house and got its own string in the village *quipu*, which registered such vital statistics as the number of children, the size of its field, the crops produced on that field, the number of animals owned. A baby brought a tax exemption for one year. Men were not liable to *mita* service within the year a child was born.

Houses were very simple: an oblong of stone, with a thatched roof; mats to eat and sleep on; niches in the walls for pottery bowls and plates, wooden spoons, stone or metal knives. Cooking was done on a stone hearth with round holes, like burners on a range. Wood served for fuel and Inca women prided themselves on how economical they could be with it. The Inca were shocked at the wasteful uses of wood they observed in the Spaniards, who thought

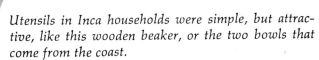

Utensils in Inca households were simple, but attractive, like this wooden beaker, or the two bowls that come from the coast.

nothing of starting large bonfires for cooking, warmth or just entertainment.

Inca diet was plain but well balanced. Meat came mainly from the llama, and was either cured and dried or cooked in a stew, with vegetables and potatoes. Guinea pigs were also used for meat, but they were considered a delicacy. The Incas cultivated corn, but used it primarily as a beverage. Their main staple was the potato, which they grew in great variety. They still do. In a highland village in Peru, you can find a dozen different potatoes each market day, ranging from small, hard, and pink to large, yellow, and soft. The highland people of the Andes were the original cultivators of the potato, one of the crops to reach Europe from the Americas.

The Incas' spices were red pepper and salt. Salt was not granulated or powdered. It was put on the family eating mat in the form of a crystal, and everyone had a lick to sharpen their palate before they dug into their bowl of stew.

Broth was prepared from quinoa leaves and oca roots, and Inca families washed their meal down with mulberry juice or another high-vitamin drink made from the leaves of the maguey plant. For special occasions, they had *chicha*, a beer brewed from corn, or *viñapa*, a hard liquor also distilled from corn.

They did have three kinds of bread: one for daily use; one for special occasions; and a third, baked with blood, for ritual purposes.

Clothes were simple as well. Women made them at home, of wool in the highlands, cotton in the lowlands, lengths of which were issued to them by the government each year. The men's basic garments were a breechclout; a short poncho that served as a com-

Clothes were sensible but appealing,
like this woolen cap.
PHOTOGRAPH BY CHARLES UHT. COURTESY OF
THE MUSEUM OF PRIMITIVE ART, NEW YORK

Women made clothes at home with
weaving implements such as these of
wood, stone, metal, shell, bamboo,
and bone.
PHOTOGRAPH BY CHARLES UHT. COURTESY OF
THE MUSEUM OF PRIMITIVE ART, NEW YORK

Inca purics *were not allowed to hunt animals, except on special occasions, but they were permitted to catch birds that threatened the harvest.*
COURTESY OF THE AMERICAN MUSEUM OF NATURAL HISTORY

bination shirt-tunic; and, for special occasions or when it was very cold, a mantle. Completing the costume were sandals, a woolen pouch that was carried slung over the shoulder, and around the head a ribbon or, on cold days, a woolen cap with earflaps.

Women wore a long tunic, with a belt; a shawl that was crossed in front and held in place with a pin, but could, in the cold weather, also be used as a head-covering. Sandals, usually made of wool, completed the women's costume.

Every individual had two outfits, one for every day and one for special occasions.

A minimal individuality could be displayed through the use of cosmetics—women apparently knew how to make and use rouge—and men of the nobility wore earrings and other jewelry. Women were not allowed to do much with their hair. They wore it long, parted in the middle and hanging down the back in two plaits. Men were even more restricted. Their hair just hung and was kept fairly short. Length of hair indicated social status. The higher the status, the shorter the hair. A crew cut indicated a member of the ruling family.

What did an Inca family do other than work? Not very much. It

In the cold highlands, wool was worked into shoulder bags and four-pointed caps that could be pulled over the ears.
THE METROPOLITAN MUSEUM OF ART, GIFT OF GEORGE D. PRATT, 1932 (Left)
THE METROPOLITAN MUSEUM OF ART, GIFT OF GEORGE D. PRATT, 1933 (Right)

attended public festivities, which were quite numerous. Each month had its own festival, and large celebrations were held for solstice and equinox every year. In addition, state occasions were proclaimed by the Inca to celebrate the birth of a prince, a major victory in war, or some other event that struck the ruling Inca's fancy. On such occasions, work was called off for the day. People dressed in their holiday clothes; watched their priests sacrifice a llama and read the future from its entrails; danced; listened to presumably uplifting speeches from their governors; drank a lot of *chicha*; and, if it was a religious festival, chewed *coca*, the pain-killing, euphoria-inducing narcotic that, at such times, was doled out to them in small quantities to help bring their spirits closer to the evanescent glow of the sun.

V   CUZCO,
THE GOLDEN CAPITAL

In Cuzco, the golden capital of the Inca empire, festivities were more elaborate and splendid than in any other place of the Inca realm. Cuzco really was golden. Its streets were narrow and the high-walled buildings made them look like canyons, but some of these walls actually were sheathed in gold. When the empire was at its apex, the ruling Incas gold-plated their palaces, and Cuzco's main sanctuary, the fabled Temple of the Sun, had gardens in which everything—trees and grass and flowers, animals, birds, butterflies, cornstalks and quinoa roots, snakes, lizards and snails were hammered gold. In Cuzco, located at close to thirteen thousand feet, the air is crisp and clear and the sun reflecting on all that gold must have been a truly dazzling sight. Even the conquistadors, to whom Spain was the measure of all things superior, thought Cuzco magnificent.

Pedro Sancho, secretary to the conqueror of Peru, Francisco Pizarro, and "scrivener" to Pizarro's army, in a very bare-boned report to Madrid, entitled simply: *An Account of the Conquest of*

Cuzco, the golden capital, was guarded by the massive fortress of Sacsahuaman.
NOEL WERRETT

Peru wrote of Cuzco: "The City of Cuzco is the principal one of all those where the lords of this land have their residence. It is so large, and so beautiful, that it would be worthy of admiration even in Spain."

The people of Cuzco thought of their city as a puma, which was a sacred animal. They conceived the city proper, enclosed between the torrents of two rivers, as the puma's body, while its head was the powerful fortress of Sacsahuaman, a mammoth, labyrinthian structure of huge rocks that stands to this day.

Cuzco radiated from a central square, known as *haucaipate*, the square of festival, or the square of joy, into four quarters named: hummingbird, lizard, salt window, and tobacco field. Each quarter represented its part of the empire, with vassal princes and adminis-trators from their respective countries in permanent or temporary residence. A prince from Nazca, for example, in residence in Cuzco, would live in the southwestern quarter of the city, while an ad-ministrator back from Quito to render report would be housed in the northeastern quarter. Cuzco was, in fact, a political map of the empire and the Incas thought of their capital as "the navel of the world." In Quechua, the imperial language of the Incas, *cosco* means navel.

In this golden navel of a city, the most important festival of the year was the Capac Inti Raimi, the King Sun Festival, which was the celebration of the summer solstice. Since Peru lies south of the equator, the summer solstice falls on December 22, and to the Incas this was the beginning of the year. It began with a three-day fast and ablution in which everyone, from the reigning Inca to the humblest street-sweeper, took part. The night preceding the solstice, December 21, the entire populace spent on their knees facing east, watching and praying for the sun to rise. When it did, the reigning Inca flung up both his arms in a gesture that was part triumphant salute and part embrace of his father, the sun. The Inca then held out to his "father" a consecrated, golden cup of *chicha* which, once the sun's rays had made it sparkle, the Inca drained. To the awed spectators, this sealed a compact between the sun and their Inca, promising that the sun would run its course for the following year, would appear as needed for light, for warmth, for crops.

Later, after the priests had offered animal sacrifices, the Inca would share these burned offerings and more of the consecrated *chicha* with men of the empire whom he wished to honor: members of his own family to whom he wanted to draw attention; members of the lower nobility who had given outstanding service; military men who had distinguished themselves in combat; or foreign princes whom he wanted to reward either because they had proven particularly faithful allies, or because he thought public homage might make them feel closer to the empire.

It was all done with great finesse. When the Inca offered a drink to another person, two golden vessels of exactly equal size were used, both containing the exact same amount of *chicha*. The man thus honored was allowed to keep his cup.

For the King Sun Festival, lords, *curacas* and vassals poured into Cuzco from all over the empire, wearing for the occasion their native costumes and particularly the headdress of their home province. Garcilaso de la Vega describes the scene:

The *curacas* came to the ceremony in their finest array with garments and headdress richly ornamented with gold and silver.

Others, who claimed to descend from a lion, appeared, like Hercules himself, wearing the skin of this animal on their backs, and on their heads, its head.

Others still, came got up as one imagines angels, with the great wings of the bird called condor, which they considered their original ancestor.

All the *curacas* in the region came too, decorated or made up to symbolize their armorial bearings. Each nation presented its weapons: bows and arrows, lances, darts, slings, maces and hatchets, both short and long according to whether they used them with one hand or two.

They also carried paintings, representing feats they had accomplished in the service of the sun and of the Inca, and whole retinues of musicians played on the timpani and trumpets they had brought with them. In other words, it may be said that each nation came to the feast with everything that could serve to enhance its renown and distinction and, if possible, its precedence over the others.

While the attendant nobility was making its political points, and the Inca bestowed his political rewards, the people celebrated in their own way. They, too, had music: flutes, drums and trumpets; and with this band striking up, the people joined in a rhythmic, stately and repetitive series of steps. There was little passion or joy in these dances, and no abandon. They were grave rituals, another form of obeisance to the Inca and to the system.

"We know the pattern," the people were saying with their dance, "and we perform as commanded."

What lightness of spirit such celebrations did contain appeared later on, when food was distributed to everyone, *chicha* flowed freely, and there was happiness in all hearts at the knowledge that the high priest, the ruling Inca's brother, had caught a sliver of the sun, lit a fire with it, and that fire was now burning securely in the Holy of Holies of Coricancha.

Coricancha, Cuzco's Temple of the Sun, was the most revered shrine in the empire. Its mystical status was such that if two persons met on a road and one of them came from Cuzco, the other one would immediately greet him as a superior simply because he had been in the vicinity of Coricancha. All reigning Incas "vied with each other in ornamenting it with incredible wealth, each Inca surpassing his successor."

These two observations come once again from Garcilaso de la Vega who also says that Corichanca means "the place of gold" and, describing it, explains why it was given that name.

The main room of the temple, Garcilaso reports, held the high altar which was dedicated to the sun. It stood facing east. The four walls of that room

> were hung with plaques of gold, from top to bottom, and a likeness of the sun topped the high altar. The likeness was made of a gold plaque twice as thick as those that paneled the walls and was composed of a

round face, prolonged by rays and flames. . . . The whole thing was so immense that it occupied the entire back of the temple, from one wall to the other. . . .

On either side of this sun were kept the numerous mummies of former Inca kings which were so well preserved that they seemed to be alive. They were seated on their golden thrones resting on plaques of this same metal and they looked directly at the visitor. . . .

The temple was prolonged by a square cloister with an adjoining wall and crowned by a gold band. . . . The three other sides of the cloister gave on to five large square rooms that had no communication between them and were roofed over in the form of a pyramid.

The first of these rooms was dedicated to the moon, the bride of the sun, and for this reason it was nearest to the main building. It was entirely paneled with silver and a likeness of the moon, with the face of a woman, decorated it in the same way that the sun decorated the larger building. . . . The bodies of queens were laid away in this temple just as those of the kings were kept in the other. . . .

The room nearest that of the moon was devoted to Venus, to the Pleiades and to all the stars. . . . This room was hung with silver, like that of the moon and the ceiling was dotted with stars, like the firmament.

The next room was dedicated to lightning and to thunder. This room was entirely covered with gold. . . .

The fourth room was devoted to the rainbow, which they said had descended from the sun, and which figured on the scutcheon of the Inca kings. It was entirely covered with gold and the rainbow was painted, in beautiful colors, across the entire surface of one of the walls.

The fifth and last room was reserved for the high priest and his assistants who were all of royal blood. . . .

The reigning Inca's private quarters were similarly gold-studded. Outer and inner walls were sheathed in gold and the Inca's palace had a golden garden similar to that of the Temple of the Sun. When receiving visitors, the Inca sat on a golden stool. He took his meals from golden platters, his drink from golden goblets.

Otherwise, the Inca's daily living pattern was not very different from those of his subjects. He wore the same clothes—breech-clout, tunic, mantle, shoulder pouch and hairband—except that the Inca's clothes were of fine vicuña wool, while his subjects' were made of the coarser fibers of the llama or the alpaca. The Inca's garments were woven and sewn by Chosen Women and, unlike his subjects, who wore their two suits of clothing until the garments fell apart, the Inca never donned a garment more than once. The Inca's clothes were carefully collected each night and, along with any food or drink that he had touched but not finished, were stored

The Inca, in his royal robe and borla, carrying his
mace, a golden star mounted on a golden rod.

and ceremoniously burned once a year. The only item of clothing unique to the Inca was the *borla,* a wide band around the forehead with crimson tassles dangling from golden tubes. The *borla* was the Inca equivalent to the European king's crown. Other members of the high nobility also wore *borlas* on special occasions, but theirs were of a different color. Crimson was reserved for the ruler. In public the Inca also carried a mace—a gold star mounted on a golden rod—and was attended by two color guards also carrying maces. On state occasions the Inca was attended by a standard bearer who carried the royal flag, a small square pennant, heavily covered in paint to make it stiff, displaying in even heavier paint the arms of the reigning Inca.

The Inca's food differed from his subjects in that his choice was wider. He had wild duck and partridge, frogs and snails, fish and seafood from the coast, and tropical fruit from the trans-Andean lands. But, like his subjects, he ate only two meals a day, one in the morning, on rising, and one at dusk.

Also like his subjects, the Inca slept on the floor, on a cotton quilt covered with sheets. The Inca's sheets, however, were vicuña rather than the coarser wool of other animals, or the cotton that was used on the coast.

No private dwelling in the Inca empire had a door, including the palace. The entryway to the Inca's residence was covered with a vicuña hanging, embroidered with feathers. Less illustrious citizens were not allowed to cover their entryways—dwellings had to be easily open to inspection at all times—but when privacy was essential they indicated the fact by hanging a bundle of feathers from the roof.

Situated immediately behind the palace was the princely academy, the only school for boys in the Inca empire. It was open to the nobility including the sons of rulers from every part of the empire. In this way, the Incas made certain that the young princes of their vassal states were thoroughly steeped in the Inca way of life: its thought and action, belief and behavior, skills and knowledge, discipline and character. A graduate of the Cuzco academy was a perfect specimen of Inca civilization.

The school offered courses in every subject a prince needed to govern in the Inca empire. The academy taught religion, for example, not as theology or doctrine, but as a calendric method so that princes could themselves calculate the seasons and the coincidence of the solar and lunar year, and thereby check on the priests whose official task it was to make these calculations and proclaim them. The princes were also taught the detail of religious ritual and its political implications and uses.

Another subject, history, was really a form of highly dramatic and effective brainwashing. Academy teachers, *amautas*, presented to the students painted boards depicting highlights of Inca history and accompanied this visual presentation with a recitation, in verse and rhyme, of the event. It was, of course, highly selective history they taught in this fashion, and since there were no written records of any kind, Inca history is more suspect in terms of factual accuracy than other histories of that time.

Another subject taught at the academy was language. The various peoples of the Inca empire spoke a great variety of tongues and the Inca realized early that language is a vital ingredient of political unity. Their native speech belonged to the language group known as Quechua and they saw to it that in all parts of the empire any-

Inca nobles drank from silver beakers.
PHOTOGRAPH BY CHARLES UHT. COURTESY OF
THE MUSEUM OF PRIMITIVE ART, NEW YORK

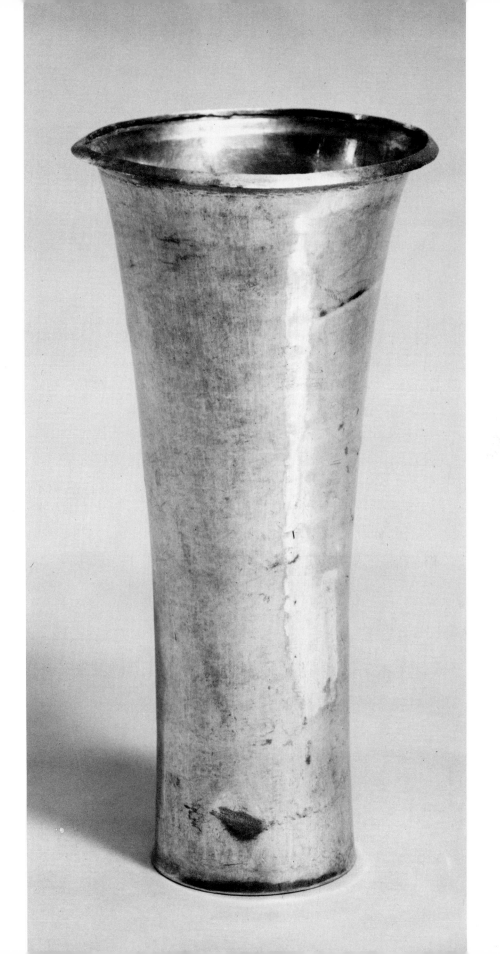

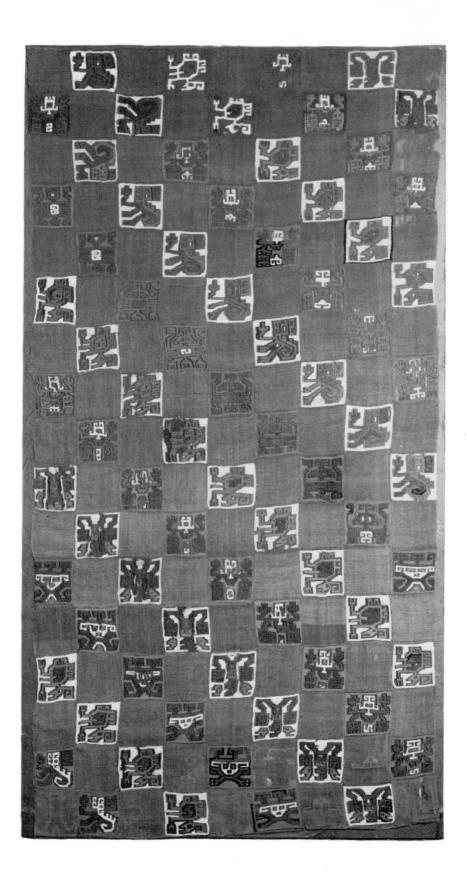

one of importance learned to speak Quechua. As a result, the Incas' tribal tongue became what Latin was to the Roman empire, French to diplomacy in the nineteenth century, and what English is today to the world of business. If you wanted to belong, you had to learn it. At the Cuzco academy, the foreign princes learned it to perfection.

The fourth major subject at the academy was statistics, the manipulation of the *quipu*, the adding machine on strings that played such an important part in the effective administration of the Inca empire. While princes would have no occasion to knot a *quipu* themselves, the Inca thought it advisable that princes know enough about the science to understand how it worked. The Inca system had *quipu* specialists much like modern corporations have accountants, but it was as vital for a prince to be able to read a *quipu* as it is for a corporation president to read a balance sheet.

Two other major study areas at the academy covered the arts of war and peace. Princes learned how to map military campaigns and execute them. This included in-the-field training. They learned as well what to do with a territory once it had been conquered, from the introduction of Inca systems of administration and production to such concrete detail as land surveys and the making of model relief maps.

To enforce discipline, academy teachers were allowed to cane obstreperous princes, but no more than once a day and only on the soles of the feet.

Princes graduated from the academy at age sixteen, when they had to pass a tough final examination called *huaracu*. Graduation ceremonies included a very demanding series of physical tests and doubled as an initiation into adult life. The combination of mental

Wall hangings like this one also served as doors.
PHOTOGRAPH BY CHARLES UHT. COURTESY OF
THE MUSEUM OF PRIMITIVE ART, NEW YORK

and physical requirements seems to have been as rigorous as that of the classic Greeks, except that the Incas' intellectual challenges were always practical, never speculative, and the purpose of the entire exercise was not to produce the complete man, but the man capable of effectively exercising power.

An equivalent institution existed for women. Special officials scoured the empire once a year for the most appealing girls of the kingdom. These Chosen Women were sent to convent schools at age twelve. In these schools, *mamacunas*, Chosen Women of a previous generation, instructed them in domestic and religious arts. The domestic arts included spinning, weaving, tie dyeing, painting, featherwork, embroidery and the preparation of meals. The religious arts included ritual dances, the preparation of the sacred bread that was used on ceremonial occasions, and of the consecrated *chicha* which was brewed in a traditional manner. On graduation, girls became either wives or concubines of the nobility, or Virgins of the Sun, celibates with religious obligations that involved the tending of temples and of the sacred fire that burned in each sanctuary of the empire, as a kind of local representative of the sun.

Except for a male overseer, who had to be of the royal family, the convent schools were run entirely by women. The daily routine in these institutions was demanding and the basic pattern of existence austere, but the convents were lavishly furnished and endowed. The all-observing Garcilaso says that in Cuzco, the tableware of the House of Chosen Women

> was either of gold or silver. They [the women] also
> had the privileges of a garden of precious metals,

*"Chosen Women" ate and drank from silver dishes
like these vessels and bowl.*
PHOTOGRAPHS BY CHARLES UHT. COURTESY OF
THE MUSEUM OF PRIMITIVE ART, NEW YORK

similar to that of the temple [of the sun]; for being wives of the sun, it was required that they be given the same treatment [as the priests] in every particular.

Garcilaso claims that such rich furnishings were customary in all convents. The reason, he says, is that "all the precious metal that was dug in the imperial mines served no other purpose than that of decorating the temples, convents and royal palaces."

According to Garcilaso, no one else in the empire could own any gold, or use it. This included all members of the nobility, higher or

Most Inca families used ceramic cups, bottles, and plates.
COURTESY OF THE AMERICAN MUSEUM OF
NATURAL HISTORY

lower. The only gold such nobles might have would be a goblet awarded them by the Inca, for special services or as a particular privilege. Gold and silver were considered sacred, with gold regarded as the sweat of the sun, silver the tears of the moon.

Whatever the charms and attractions of being a Chosen Woman, the cost of the privilege abused came high. If a Virgin of the Sun broke her vow of chastity she was buried alive and the man involved was hanged. To demonstrate the full horror of the crime, not only was the man himself hanged, but so were his wife and children if he had any, his servants and all his close relations.

"And in order that the punishment should be complete," the meticulous Garcilaso adds, "his cattle were also to be put to death, his fields destroyed, his house razed to the ground, and the entire place was to be strewn with stones so that nothing could grow there again."

The same applied to the family of the girl, and her entire *ayllu*. Inca fiction that has survived from the imperial days—epic poems and plays—concern tragedy caused by romantic entanglements between Chosen Women and men they loved or who loved them. Possibly these stories were altered, in structure or interpretation, by the Spaniards who heard and recorded them. The conquistadors were, after all, nourished on the romances of medieval Europe and were partial to tales of romantic devotion.

Garcilaso maintains no such entanglements ever occurred. He cites the law for errant Virgins of the Sun but adds: "I do not believe that the occasion ever arose to enforce it, for the Indians had deep respect for their duty, particularly for those duties that touched upon religious beliefs."

VI MUSCLES OF EMPIRE

There is no doubt that the Inca's subjects did have a deep respect for their duties. There is also no doubt that these duties were meticulously designed and efficiently enforced. The efficiency consisted not only of technical competence but of attitudes and behavioral approaches that were, for their time and place, humane. The Inca governmental system was rational and, as systems go, elegant.

The political structure was sustained by three pillars: the civil administration, the religious hierarchy, and the military apparatus. Crowning the structure was the ruling Inca, in symbol and fact a radiant and reassuring source of power and security.

Ruling Incas had a chain of titles. They were called, predictably, "the unique Inca," an appellation not unearned when one considers the dramatic achievements of the thirteen Incas who, in succession, built, aggrandized and lost the largest empire of the Americas before the white man came. Incas were also addressed, functionally, as emperor.

Their most glorious title, and the one they occupied in the

imagination of their subjects, was "son of the sun."

But the designation that probably endeared them most to the millions of *purics*, who made possible their power, was "lover of the poor." It was a title they took seriously. The Inca were perhaps the first to realize the political truth that a society is no stronger than its weakest link.

The Inca's wife who, as in ancient Egypt, was frequently his sister, was officially called *coya*, meaning empress. Her more popular title, however, and the one which both caused and expressed the affection with which her subjects regarded her, was *mamanic*, our mother.

Special titles designated other members of the reigning family, that is, all who were Incas by physical descent from Manco Capac and Mama Ocla. A conquistador reports that there were five hundred of these by the time he encountered them. Young princes, boys that had not yet undergone their graduation initiation from the royal academy, were called *awkis*. After graduation, they became *incas*. For girls of the royal family, titles depended on their marital state. Unmarried, they were *nyostas;* married they became *palyas*, which the Spaniards translated as ladies.

Only direct descendants of the first Inca could become members of the highest body of civil government in the empire, the State Council. That body resembled a combination of the British Privy Council and the United States National Security Agency. Its members reported directly to the Inca and their main task was to brief him on the state of the empire and to carry out his wishes for the empire; that is, to see that his orders, on large matters or small, were known and executed throughout the realm.

The council consisted of the prefects of the four quarters that made up the empire, plus a secretary. These prefects resided in Cuzco and, while they were invariably Incas by direct descent, the posts were not hereditary. They were assigned by the reigning Inca according to merit.

The prefects had counterparts who lived within their constituencies. These were the imperial governors, *toqrikoq*, who constituted the supreme civilian authority in what was called provinces, equivalent to the states in the political structure of the United States.

The Incas tried to have provinces correspond as much as possible to the native kingdoms they had added to the empire, or to tribal groups. However, when these were too small to fit the Inca notion of administrative efficiency, they put two or three of them together to constitute a province.

To the Incas, a province was a certain number of taxpayers, neatly fitted into a decimal system. The top taxpaying unit consisted of ten thousand persons and, to be recognized as a province, a territory had to have at least one such unit. Most provinces had between two and four. Provincial governors had to be Incas by direct descent, but their positions, too, were appointments by merit, not by heredity.

Since even the substantial group of male descendants of Manco Capac and Mama Ocla did not provide too wide a base of choice for civil administrators, every job below that of provincial governor was open to the minor nobility, whose members were called *curacas*. *Curacas* were either Incas by direct descent through the female line—which included both wives and concubines; members of royal houses who had joined the Inca empire by choice, per-

Sweeping mantles, with embroidered borders, sometimes depicted warriors at work.
PHOTOGRAPH BY CHARLES UHT. COURTESY OF
THE MUSEUM OF PRIMITIVE ART, NEW YORK

suasion or conquest; or military men whose spectacular achievements had earned them a place among the *curacas,* much like knighthood was earned in Europe during the same historic period.

Curacas administered civil government at the level of ten thousand taxpayers. An administrator in charge of a unit of that size was called a *hono curaca.* Under him served two *pica curacas,* responsible for five thousand taxpayers each. Reporting to these were *waranca curacas,* with a thousand taxpayers under their jurisdiction. Their authority, in turn, covered two *pica pachaca curacas,* with five hundred taxpayers to supervise.

All these positions were by appointment, on merit. They were exacting positions because the Inca system demanded taut competence at every level of administration and each administrator was held personally responsible for the performance and the well-being of each individual under his jurisdiction.

The material rewards were minor. A *curaca* who had done an outstanding job might be rewarded by assignment to him of one or more of the Chosen Women. He might be given some extra plots of land for his family use or a number of heads of llama. Rarer still were such personal signs of the Inca's favor as a few yards of the vicuña cloth made by the Virgins of the Sun for the Inca and his family, a featherwork tapestry for the *curaca's* house, or, most glamorous, the sharing of a drink with the Inca during·the Inti Raimi festival and the subsequent award of a gold or silver cup. The real compensation for these positions of power and responsibility were much what they are today: challenge and status.

The system changed at the lower levels of administration, beginning with the *pachaca curaca,* who was responsible for units of

The reigning Inca drank only from golden cups
and vessels, while most of his subjects used
ceramic vessels like these, made on the coast.
THE METROPOLITAN MUSEUM OF ART, GIFT OF
NATHAN CUMMINGS, 1966
PHOTOGRAPH BY CHARLES UHT. COURTESY OF
THE MUSEUM OF PRIMITIVE ART, NEW YORK

one hundred *purics*. The position of *pachaca curaca* was hereditary, subject to the Inca's approval. The reason for this was that the job was usually awarded to a local chieftain who was known and honored by his people. This built into a system that depended primarily on efficiency and responsibility an ingredient that responded to affection and respect based on intimate personal knowledge. It had all the advantages of an old-fashioned United States political machine, with none of its faults. Abuse of power was prevented by the Inca's veto if the *pachaca curaca* proved unsuitable; and his wings were clipped further by the fact that the administrators below him were once again appointed—not by him, but by the *curaca* who was his superior.

The lowest rungs of the administrative ladder consisted of *pica conka kamayok*, men in charge of fifty *purics* each, whose tasks were comparable to those of a foreman in a factory, and the littlest boss in the Inca system, *conka kamayok*, who had ten taxpayers under his charge.

The *conka kamayok* were straw bosses. Record-keeping—the basic tool of Inca efficiency—began with the *pica conka kamayok*, who kept all statistics of imperial interest: births, deaths, marriages, changes of age grades, and production figures in the fields and of the herds. The foremen turned in monthly reports, and these reports traveled on up the administrative line until they were coordinated and summarized by the provincial governor. The governor reported to the Inca himself once a year, during the Inti Raimi festival.

The system was tightly knit and practically corruption proof, but to make quite certain it functioned flawlessly the Inca set up a control mechanism, a network of inspectors who traveled the realm at all times and for a number of purposes. They searched for the Chosen Women whose beauty and character made them eligible to become *mamacunas* or Virgins of the Sun. They looked for special talents among boys and young men. They stuck their heads into *purics'* huts and *curacas'* residences to make certain all was arranged according to Inca plan. And they kept an ear to the ground to hear grievances or neglects; to check whether the law was being applied fairly and quickly; even to find out whether the clergy was properly fulfilling its duties.

These "super-snoopers" were known as *tokoyrikoq*, which means "see-all." Their assignment was to check on everybody and everything, openly or secretly. Since they snooped impartially, in all sectors and at all levels of society, and listened to grievances and complaints as well as paying unwanted surprise visits, they were probably not too unpopular. They certainly had a vital function which they seem to have discharged almost faultlessly. Corruption was practically unknown in the Inca empire, a fact that really impressed the Spaniards. For good reason: the Spaniards' own political system, and those of all Europe at the time, could make no such claim.

Civil administrators doubled as judges. They enforced the law. The process was simple and swift. Accuser and defendant would state their case and, if they had witnesses, produce them. The judge listened, decided, and awarded punishment. In minor cases he did so immediately; in more serious cases, he might take a day or two to think things over. In any case, sentence had to be passed within five days at most, unless the crime involved was beyond the administrator's jurisdiction and had to be passed up the line. This applied when the defendant was a *curaca* or when the crime called for the death penalty. Only the governor of a province, or the Inca himself, could decree the death penalty.

Law among the Incas was deliberately discriminatory. The higher a person's status in the hierarchy, the more law-respecting he was expected to be. Punishment was more severe for nobles than for the ordinary *puric* committing the same crime. Adultery, for example, which was a crime, earned the *puric*, or the *puric's* wife, a nasty session of torture. A *curaca* caught in adultery was condemned to death.

Methods of punishment also differed, the assumption being that nobles were more susceptible to psychological and social punishment than were ordinary folk. A very serious form of punishment for a *curaca* would be to expose him to public ridicule, or even just to public rebuke. Depriving a *curaca* of his office was considered as bad as exposing a *puric* to torture, and sending a *curaca* into exile to work on the trans-Andean *coca* plantations was the Inca equivalent of the French sending Captain Dreyfus to Devil's Island.

When the death penalty was applied, a *puric* was killed by blows on the head with a stone club, by having a rock dropped on his back from a height of three feet, or by being hurled off a cliff. Nobles who had earned the death penalty were thrown into a dungeon in Cuzco. The dungeon was stocked with poisonous snakes and carniverous animals that had been assembled especially for this terror- and death-dealing purpose.

For the *puric* and his wife and children, laziness was considered a misdemeanor, punishable by law. Theft was regarded as a felony,

The Incas worshipped the sun and their ruler. Other people had different deities. This is a statue that was worshipped by the Chimu.
COURTESY OF THE AMERICAN MUSEUM OF
NATURAL HISTORY

although special provision was made for theft of food. If a person had stolen food because of need, he was still punished but so was his immediate superior in the political hierarchy. The superior was held responsible for the fact that the person under his jurisdiction found himself in need.

Manslaughter in self-defense, or involving an adulterous spouse, was a felony, not a capital crime. But stealing from the fields or herds of the Inca, setting fire to bridges or storehouses, or entering a convent of Chosen Women without permission were capital crimes. Such acts involved the property of the Inca and were therefore considered not only crimes against society but blasphemy as well.

Crime seems to have been infrequent. There was little motivation for it and punishment was certain. For the average *puric*, law was reduced to a simple three-pronged injunction: "*ama sua, ama llulla, ama checklla:* do not steal, lie, be lazy." It was a simple code and obeying it was quite evidently the better part of wisdom.

The second major pillar of the Inca political edifice was the clerical hierarchy. Its structure was different from that of the civil administration and its functions distinct and separate. But it served the same basic purpose: to encourage and inspire subjects to do their duty and thereby sustain the Inca and the empire.

The top man in the clerical hierarchy was the high priest, who was always the brother of the reigning Inca, resided in Cuzco, and presided over Coricancha, the glowing, glorious Temple of the Sun. Ten bishops served under the high priest, supervising a multitude of secondary working clergymen who resided in the communities in which they served. In that sense, they were parish priests, except that they were divided into four categories, by function.

There were the ritualists, whose main job it was to instruct the community in calendric progression, specifically to tell the *ayllu* when the time had come to sow, plant, and harvest. These priests also led the rituals that accompanied these activities and gave them their spiritual dimension.

Another category of priests acted as confessors to whom the *puric* could confide his sins and get absolution. Confession took place on the shore of a river and the priest would hear it holding a fistful of *ichu* grass—the strong, hard grass of the highlands—in one hand, a stone in the other. Having heard the confession, the priest took the sin into himself, then spat it out into the *ichu* and finally threw the sin-drenched grass into the river which carried it away. Then the priestly hand that held the stone performed its part of the ritual, the priest delivering the sinner a blow, with the severity of the blow, and its location, contingent on the seriousness of the sin. A really nasty violation of moral law or religious practice could fetch a sharp blow on the back of the head that could be very painful for quite some time. A lighter offense might bring just a rap on the knuckles.

Penance was meted out in addition. The most severe was an order to "dwell in the wilderness" for a period of time, that is, religious banishment. This was quite different from the exile ordered by a civil judge. Civil exile encompassed hard labor. Religious penance required only solitude, with a man or woman foraging to keep alive and, without the supportive comfort of family and community, experiencing the pangs of loneliness and, hopefully, the stimulus to spiritual improvement that solitude might bring.

A third category of priests were the diviners, who foretold events of major concern to the community—the strength of the wind, the warmth of the sun, the size of the harvest—by reading auguries from the innards of llamas, ritually sacrificed. The Romans had a similar practice. Their priests predicted the outcome of important military campaigns by reading auguries from chicken livers.

The fourth category of priests were clerical equivalents of the political "see-alls," inspectors who checked on local temples, on parish ritual, and on the convents of Chosen Women that were spread throughout the empire.

The third major pillar of the Inca empire was the army. Like the civil administration, the military was organized on a decimal basis. It was essentially a draft army, the basic unit being the recruits of one *ayllu* who served together whenever and wherever possible. The largest military unit encompassed ten thousand soldiers, and all military officers, up to and including the commander of ten thousand, could rise from the ranks.

The Inca army fought with slings—not little peashooters but thick ropes hurling fist-sized rocks that could easily split an unprotected skull. The sling was twirled around several times before the rock was released, much like the hammer is thrown in Olympic games. This was the main long-range weapon. Up closer, the Incas fought with lances, about six feet long. For hand-to-hand fighting they used battle sticks, cudgels topped with sharp-edged stones as deadly as any bayonet. They also had a short, broad, double-edged sword of very hard wood. They protected themselves with armor of quilted cotton, wooden helmets, shields of hide held to the chest, and shields of wood fastened to the back.

Recruits joining the army needed little training in the basic skills of battle. Inca boys used slings from the age of ten and were accustomed also to the handling of knives. Manipulating a lance was a skill they did have to learn and they also had to be taught how to defend themselves against enemy missiles. The Incas themselves did not use bows and arrows. They did what the Romans did: they incorporated into their armies warriors for whom the bow and arrow were a natural weapon. In the Inca army these were the warriors from the jungles of trans-Andean lowlands.

A recruit fresh from his *ayllu* also had to learn military tactics. Inca military arts were sophisticated for their time. In their campaigns, the Incas devised strategies that cut off an enemy's communications lines for reinforcements and supplies. They simulated retreats to get the enemy saddled with longer or more difficult supply lines, and provide the Inca army with a more favorable terrain. And they preceded battle with a personal pep talk from the commander to the troops and the encouragement by officers for their men to hurl themselves into combat with morale-boosting yells and shouts, the more bloodcurdling the better. Noise-making was considered a weapon, a kind of psychological warfare, and apparently it often succeeded. In this, as in every other aspect of his conduct, the Inca soldier was superbly disciplined and his drilled, devoted keening rattled even the Spaniards. To the peoples of South America who knew the reputation of the Inca army, the sound must have been unsettling in the extreme.

A warrior, with shield and battle stick.

PHOTOGRAPH BY CHARLES UHT. COURTESY OF
THE MUSEUM OF PRIMITIVE ART, NEW YORK

A warrior depicted in the border of a Nazca mantel.
THE METROPOLITAN MUSEUM OF ART, GIFT OF
GEORGE D. PRATT, 1933

As every other political tool in the Inca empire, the efficacy of the army rested in substantial part on its concern with the men who served in it. An adage asserts that every army travels on its stomach. The Inca soldier had nothing to worry about on that score. He was supplied from the Inca's empire-wide network of storehouses, which meant that he was the best-fed, best-dressed, best-equipped soldier in the Americas. And while fighting could be rough while it lasted, Inca military methods provided for a cycle of battle not exceeding twenty days per month. The Incas usually launched their campaigns with the rising of the full moon and, unless there was a commanding need to continue, called a halt after twenty days of fighting. This guaranteed Inca troops at least ten days of rest and recuperation each month. Today's soldiers don't do as well.

Finally, Inca soldiers had the emotional security of fighting in a unit of their own *ayllu*, with men who knew each other from childhood and cared about each other. The subtlest, but perhaps most important, morale booster was the fact that every Inca soldier, down to the lowest-ranking trooper, knew that in his absence his family was taken care of, his fields tended, his animals looked after, and that he would return after the war to find everything at home exactly as he had left it.

The Inca soldier had need of high morale. He was under strictest orders not to kill unnecessarily, not to loot, rape, or offend the conquered population in any way. The Inca precept in this matter was a combination of presumption and sophistication that no other empire builders had achieved before, or have mastered since. The Inca attitude, first formulated by the Inca Pachacuti but professed and practiced by all his successors, was: "It is not well to kill and destroy, for in the end they [the conquered peoples] are all ours and we should not destroy our own."

Once fighting had ceased, the Inca army became a garrison and in that capacity considered itself the advance patrol of Inca civilization. Under its aegis, Inca skills and Inca values were introduced: first, agriculture, using fertilizers, irrigation, and terracing where needed, plus the tri-partite division of fields and their products into sun property, Inca property and personal property. Next, the establishment of storehouses, with their meticulous systems of account-keeping; roads to connect the new storage centers to the imperial network; the construction of bridges; and the fast and dependable messenger service to furnish the communication that made sound administration possible.

Wherever they went, the Incas also introduced their language, Quechua, not to supplant the local tongue but to add to it the linguistic tool that made empire-wide understanding possible. Everywhere, the Incas also introduced their worship of the sun, with all its institutions and rituals. In this sensitive area, they once again did not replace local beliefs and ceremonies; they just added to native faith the golden glow of sun worship, which must have been immensely appealing.

How appealing can perhaps be deduced from the fact that cities conquered by the Incas were never fortified. Inca garrisons customarily built a fortress on a hilltop overlooking the town, which served as the garrison's headquarters, but constituted as well a place of refuge for the town's residents in time of danger. There were no walls around cities occupied by the Incas, no moats and no

Some of the tools that made possible the Incas' "mission civilizataire": axe blades, club bends, fishline sinkers, weights—all made of stone.
COURTESY OF THE AMERICAN MUSEUM OF NATURAL HISTORY

buttressed towers. With very few exceptions, there was no need for them.

When a conquered people did feel imposed upon, and failed to recognize the bounties and privileges of belonging to the Kingdom of the Sun, the Incas used a different strategy to see to it that peace and security reigned in the realm. They moved the population that appeared to doubt Inca wisdom and resettled it in another part of the empire where it was surrounded by peoples who had accepted Inça rule. The move was made with the customary Inca dispatch, efficiency and humanity. The populations, whenever possible, were moved to lands similar in soil and climate to the ones they had known.

In the towns and villages from which such people had been moved, their places were taken by colonists, complete communities that the Incas knew to be loyal and dependable. These were known as *mitmakona* and were considered the Inca's favorite subjects. *Mitmakona* were under the civil jurisdiction of the provincial governor of their new location, but were allowed to keep the customs of their own *ayllu*, and their specific headdress, if they had one. They were given special privileges and honors, which redounded on occasion not only to the *mitmakona* themselves but to the tribal group from which they had come. Thus, a loyal highland

people that had furnished an appreciable number of *mitmakona* might be awarded fields in the lowlands, which its *purics* could work to obtain products—fruits and vegetables—that could not be grown in their own, colder climate. The highlanders got their third of the proceeds.

The *mitmakona*, for their part, thought of themselves as carrying out a civilizing mission. They felt as the Romans did about bringing their laws to the "barbarians" of Europe, Asia and Africa; the way the British regarded "the white man's burden" in the nineteenth century; or the manner in which the French conceived of their colonialism as a *"mission civilizataire."*

To one European historian in the eighteenth century, a man who had studied imperial methods in Europe and Asia, the Incas seemed the acme of state-craft. Admiringly, he writes:

> The Inca were a set of men half missionaries and half conquerors: They preached sword in hand, and fought with the pastoral staff . . . They found means to unite the priesthood and the empire, the sceptre and the censer, the humanity of government and the terror of arms, the pomp of the Eastern monarchs and the popularity of the Kings of Europe.

VII SINEWS OF EMPIRE

We would not today think of Europe's kings as having been popular, although the pomp of the monarchs of the East still retains its gaudy repute. But such judgments are relative, rooted in their time and place, and compared to the political alternatives available, the kings of Europe were popular in their day. This is even more true about the Inca rulers, who were objects of love and adoration and, in their fashion, worked hard at earning both.

What the Inca kings offered to people under their rule was a set of solid accomplishments that contributed not only to the power and cohesion of the Inca empire—which they also did—but constituted as well a major improvement in the physical and emotional welfare of just about everyone in the Inca realm.

The most fundamental of these accomplishments was agricultural know-how. This consisted essentially of three ingredients, none novel in itself, but in combination and in the systematic introduction and application of the combination, unprecedented. The Incas were masters at terracing mountainsides for the effective

The Incas were expert agriculturists and their terracing and irrigation methods have survived to this day. This is typical Inca terracing on the steep mountain sides of an Andean peak.

COURTESY OF THE AMERICAN MUSEUM OF
NATURAL HISTORY

Inca irrigation methods were simple but superbly functional, like this water pipe constructed of logs.
NOEL WERRETT

growing of crops. Other civilizations, in other lands, had done it before them. But no civilization anywhere had reached quite the perfection of method or the extent to which man was pitted against parsimonious nature, and still managed to get his way. In the Andean highlands under Inca rule, mountainsides were cultivated to heights of almost three miles, which is just about the upper limit of the tree line. You can see such terraces in Peru today, and the sight is impressive still.

These fields high up in the Andes seem like sculptures on the face of the mountain: geometric designs of lines and quarter circles, squares and oblongs which, when the fields are green and glistening with an early morning dew, look like necklaces strung across the bare brown chest of the Andes.

The second ingredient of Inca agricultural know-how—irrigation —was also not an original discovery. Some of the coastal civilizations that preceded the Incas had been great irrigators, mainly because they had to be in that bone-dry expanse of sand dunes that stretches from the Pacific coast to the Andean foothills. But the Incas improved on the irrigation of their predecessors on the coast and, more important, systematized it. Before the Incas, irrigation had depended on the knowledge and whim of a particular chieftain. As a result, some valleys on the coast had excellent canals, others had barely adequate ones, and still others had none. The Incas introduced irrigation wherever it was needed to get maximum production. They also deepened existing aqueducts so that farmers could count on water at all times. One measure of Inca efficiency is the fact that under the Incas twice as much of the Peruvian coastal land was under cultivation than is in use today.

The third ingredient of the Incas' "green revolution" was fertilizer. Their contribution was that in each of the three major geographic and climatic areas of their realm—the coast, the plateaus east and west of the Andes, and the highlands—they used materials closest to hand to make fertilizer and, when local sources proved insufficient, provided the needed "import" from other parts of the empire.

We have details once again from that great collector of Inca habits and practices, Garcilaso de la Vega.

> The fertilizers they used differed according to the region. In the Cuzco valley and its environs, the corn fields were fertilized with human manure which the Indians considered to be matchless for cultivating this particular plant. They collected it carefully throughout the year, dried it and then kept it in powdered form.
>
> In the *colla* [the upper reaches of the highlands, at twelve thousand feet and more] where it is too cold to grow corn, the potato fields, which extended over more than one hundred and fifty leagues of land, were enriched with animal manure.
>
> Along the entire coast, the only fertilizer used was that of the seagulls, unbelievably numerous flocks of which were to be found there. These birds, both large and small, live on islands not far from the shore, which are covered with such quantities of their droppings that they look like mountains of snow. Under

Inca rule, the birds were protected by very severe laws: it was forbidden to kill a single one of them, or even to approach their islands during the laying season, under penalty of death.

Garcilaso's accuracy on this point is easily confirmed. To this day, the highland Indians of the Andes use animal fertilizer for their potatoes; the Indians around Cuzco employ human manure; and the rest of the country—excepting the very large plantations that import synthetic fertilizer—rely on those snow-white bird droppings, known now as *guano*. And while the death penalty does not apply anymore to anyone poaching on these sea gull islands, national law forbids access to them except by special government permit, and the collection and sale of *guano* is a government monopoly.

The Incas' know-how was not limited to agriculture. It also covered the other major source of economic welfare at the time: animal husbandry. In Inca society, the llama played a role similar to that of cattle in the United States today. Llama herds were assigned to *ayllus*, were communally tended, and tended most carefully. The first adult tasks Inca boys—and girls—were assigned, was the care of flocks. For them, it was like learning the alphabet. The Inca introduced flock care on a systematic basis to every tribe or group under their control.

They also had a negative technique of animal husbandry, designed to make certain that hunting did not decimate species of animals. As usual, their method was simple, high-handed and effective. Its basis was a law which prohibited anyone in the Inca empire from killing animals, except wild animals invading farm-lands, and certain small birds that were considered marginal to the Inca economy.

This law could have resulted in animals running wild, multiply-ing beyond control and not being available to the Inca economy. That, of course, was not the Inca way. Instead, the Incas organized an annual hunt, led by the reigning Inca himself, and pursued under total government control.

Garcilaso describes it:

Every year the Inca kings organized a great cere-monial hunt called *chacu,* which means stop, the method they employed being to group, then stop their game. . . .

The great annual royal hunt took place shortly after the mating season. In the province chosen for that year, the Inca first assembled some twenty to thirty thousand Indians. He then divided them in two groups whose duty it was to walk in circular formation across the fields and prairies, rivers and mountains, over a tract of land about twenty or thirty leagues long. As they advanced, these men headed off all the animals they came upon, forcing them back toward the middle of the circle with shouts and clapping of hands. Then the circle of beaters began to close in on the creatures who, by now, were im-prisoned as though between four walls of human bodies so that it soon became possible to catch them

*The great annual royal hunt caught in its tightly or-
ganized net every kind of animal in the empire including birds, like the raven heading this effigy vessel . . .*
PHOTOGRAPH BY CHARLES UHT. COURTESY OF
THE MUSEUM OF PRIMITIVE ART, NEW YORK

by hand. Included among them were lions, bears, foxes, and species of lynx they call *ozcollo* and all kinds of other harmful beasts. I have not mentioned tigers which one scarcely ever encounters in Peru except in the wild Andes Mountains. But roe deer, deer, and the game animals called guanacos and vicuñas were caught in vast quantities; indeed, there were sometimes as many as thirty to forty thousand head of them, and one can imagine what a magnificent spectacle they presented, huddled together that way. . . .

The game collected in this manner was sorted, and the females of an age to bear young were freed along with the finest specimens among the males, while old or ungainly animals were killed and their meat divided among the ordinary people. The guanacos and vicuñas, however, were sheared before they were set free. Meanwhile, a complete census of all this game was taken, according to sex and species and the figures were noted down by means of *quipus*.

All the guanaco wool, which is coarse in quality, was distributed among the people; while that of the vicuñas, which is the finest in the world, was sent to the royal stores, and only the Inca or those whom he expressly granted this favor, had the right to wear it. Indeed any infraction of this law was punishable by death. But the meat of the guanacos and vicuñas that were killed was also divided among the people.

. . . and deer, depicted here in a sitting posture.
THE METROPOLITAN MUSEUM OF ART, GIFT OF
NATHAN CUMMINGS, 1963

These hunts took place in each district every four years, in order to give the game time to reproduce and also to allow the vicuñas and guanacos time to grow new wool.

This "royal hunt" was a perfect example of the Inca economic system: methodical production, including the application of safeguards, designed for maximum output; and equally methodical distribution, along neatly drawn and perfectly structured hierarchical lines.

Just as the Incas' unprecedented production was made possible by a package of techniques, so was their distribution, with the distribution system perhaps the more innovative in both concept and execution.

The kingpins in the Inca distribution system (and the phenomenal sense of physical security it generated) were royal storage houses scattered throughout the empire. They were called *piruas*, were made of baked earth, with straw roofs, and located wherever possible in a high, dry place. Several structures were built in a row, with narrow alleyways between them for loading and unloading. One wall had a grating of square peepholes, about two fingers in width, through which an inspector could see at a glance the quantity of stores in a *pirua*, and the condition of these stores. In the major storehouse complexes, separate structures held grains, hides, wool, cotton, dried meat, and weapons. *Piruas* were designed for use in peace and war.

For their economic and social usefulness—the delivery of their contents when and where needed—the storage units were dependent on roads, a fact of which the Incas were thoroughly aware. The Inca road system excited the admiration of everyone who encountered it; even today it still elicits amazement from travelers, and superlatives from experts. The only roads comparable in all of human history until modern times were those of the Romans, and Roman roads had fewer obstacles to overcome. The highest Inca road was built at an altitude of over seventeen thousand feet. The longest Roman road, running from Hadrian's Wall in Scotland to the Temple in Jerusalem, was shorter than the Royal Road of the Inca, the empire's main highway, which stretched from just north of the equator to 35° latitude south, a total of 3,250 miles. The empire's second major highway ran along the coast, for a total of 2,520 miles. A network of lateral roads connected the two highways, some designed for specific purposes such as the transport of gold, military use, or what today we would call farm-to-market roads, except in Inca days these roads led from *ayllus* to *piruas*. The explorer-writer Victor von Hagen, who organized full-scale expeditions tracking the road systems of the Incas as well as of the Romans, says that the Inca Royal Road was, until the nineteenth century, the longest arterial road in the history of mankind.

The Royal Road varied in width from fifteen feet to eighteen feet but the coastal road was a uniform twenty-four feet, and was protected by sidewalls to keep out the drifting sand.

The Roman parallel seems to leap to mind whenever experts encounter the Inca road system. Count Humboldt, the eighteenth century German explorer after whom the Humboldt Current is named, said after traveling along the highways of the Incas: "Nothing I have seen among the fine Roman roads of Italy, Spain or the south of France was more imposing than these works of the ancient Peruvians."

Commenting from a different vantage point in both time and space, one of the early conquistadors, Cieza de León, a good and usually very factual observer to whom we owe considerable knowledge of Inca ways, exclaims on first encountering the Inca Royal Road: "Charles V in all his splendor would not be in a position to carry out such a work." From a Spanish knight, to whom the Emperor Charles V of Spain was the last word in royal competence and glory, this was high praise indeed.

You can almost see Cieza de León shake his conquistadorial head as he elaborates on these amazing roads and describes how they were built:

> I will explain the ease with which they were constructed by the Indians without increasing the death rate or causing excessive labor. When the Inca decided to have one of these famous roads constructed much preparation was unnecessary; it remained but for the Inca to give orders. For then the overseers went over the ground, made the trace of the road, and the Indians received instructions to construct the road using local labor. Each province completed the section of the road within its own limits; when it reached the end of their boundary, it was taken up by others; when it was urgent, all worked at the same time.

The overseers to whom Cieza de León refers were trained Inca

Kingdom of the Sun

surveyors. Land surveying was an important Inca skill. All princes were taught it in their academy in Cuzco. And road building was one portion of an *ayllu's mita*, the tax decreed by the Inca each year.

While there was considerable science in the construction of Inca roads, there was little art. Wherever possible, roads ran straight as an arrow on the principle that this was most efficient, a straight line being the shortest distance between two points. Inca roads were designed strictly for efficiency. Long stretches of them were just hard-packed, damped-down, all-weather surfaces. Some were paved causeways, usually near the cities. The paving was a composit called *pirca*, a mixture of clay, pebbles and maize leaves.

The Incas had no reason to design their roads for any purpose other than maximum efficiency because no one was allowed to use them except on government business. As one Peruvianist notes, drily, "this had the beneficial result of keeping people on the land and the roads free." Garcilaso, commenting on the practice, and as usual approving of his Inca ancestors' ways, notes that "this was in line with the first principle of Inca government: namely that each man should live in one spot, and never move from it, since vagrancy makes ne'er-do-wells and disturbs the peace." However technically accomplished the Inca highway system was, it was emphatically not an open road.

Those who traveled it on government business, however, lacked nothing. Inns were built along the roads' edge at regular intervals, with separate quarters for people and animals, and provisions for both. The inns were called *tampus*, a word still used in Peru, changed to the softer *tambo*. But while in today's Peru a traveler would have problems finding a convenient *tambo* outside the big cities and major tourist spots, in Inca days *tampus* flanked the roads at predictable distances of one day's journey. In flat terrain, where the going was easy, the Incas figured this distance to be eighteen miles, while in the highlands, where the going could be rough, *tampus* were spaced twelve miles apart. This was based on a kind of concensus calculation involving man, beast and conveyance. Man in Inca days traveled on foot. Cargo was hauled by llamas. The only conveyances to be seen on Inca highways were litters, carrying either the Inca himself, members of the royal family, or *curacas* of senior status.

Completing the Inca distribution network of storage centers, roads, inns, and transport, were bridges, most of them suspension bridges that have elicited as much respect and even awe from observers as have the roads themselves. The Incas called bridges "little brothers of the road" and considered them vital to the empire. Tampering with a bridge in any way whatever earned a saboteur the death penalty.

Most famous among Inca bridges was the one spanning the Apurimac River. Its repute has come down to us in history and literature as the bridge of San Luis Rey. It was in fact built by the second Inca, Inca Roca, and endured some five hundred years. Swaying over a precipitous gorge, with a rushing river at the bottom, it was a miracle of balanced ropes, anchored to rock on both sides of the ravine. Crossing it was an experience of excitement or horror, depending on the traveler's personality.

Pizarro's secretary, Pedro Sancho, gives a neat account of how such suspension bridges were made, and what crossing them was like.

Drawing of an Inca suspension bridge. The Inca called these bridges "little brothers of the road."
COURTESY OF THE AMERICAN MUSEUM OF
NATURAL HISTORY

If the two banks of the river are strong, they [the Inca] raise upon them large walls of stone, then they place four ropes of pliable reeds two palms or a little less in thickness, and between them after the fashion of wattle-work, they weave green osiers two fingers thick and well intertwined, in such a way that some are not left more slack than others and all are well tied. And upon these, they place branches cross-wise in such a way that the water is not seen and in this way they make the floor of the bridge. And in the same manner they weave a balustrade of these same osiers along the side of the bridge so that no one may fall into the water, of which, in truth, there is no danger, although to one who is not used to it the matter of crossing appears a thing of danger because, the span being long, the bridge bends when one goes over it so that one goes continually downward until the middle is reached, and from there he keeps going until he has finished crossing to the other bank. And when the bridge is being crossed it trembles very much so that it goes to the head of him who is not accustomed to it.

The experience certainly went to the heads of the first Spaniards who crossed an Inca bridge. Their letters home are replete with the horror of crossing the Apurimac River. The Spaniards' horses tore the weave in some places, although they did not make holes large enough for any conquistador to fall through. But many Spaniards visualized the possibility. A number of the less brave conquistadors, reports say, crawled across on their hands and knees.

At either side of the suspension bridges, the Incas had stations for a team of watchmen and repairmen who, in Pedro Sancho's picturesque description, "always have in their hands osiers and wattles and cords in order to mend the bridges if they are injured or even to rebuild them if need were."

They must have had quite a repair job on their hands after that Spanish cavalry got across.

Building and maintaining bridges was another facet of the *mita*. It was levied on the people of the community in whose territory the bridge was constructed.

Less elaborate suspension bridges existed as well, consisting at minimum of a simple rope-cable, anchored on both sides of a river or ravine. A man would have to swing across hand over hand. The Spaniards never tried one of those.

The Incas' technical accomplishments in production and distribution required an administrative underpinning to make certain the knowledge served desired social and political ends. As empire builders of incontestable genius, the Inca came up with two innovations: one in communications, the other in statistics.

Communications were handled by relay messengers called *chasquis*. They were stationed on all the roads, spaced to span a distance that could be covered by a young man in perfect physical condition at his top speed.

Chasquis were posted on raised platforms from which they observed the road in both directions. The moment they spied another messenger, they took off to meet him and, running along-

side, took his message so that not a moment would be lost. *Chasquis* lived in little huts next to their platforms, in groups of four to ten, depending on how much communications traffic was likely to come their way. They served fifteen-day shifts.

The word *chasqui*, Garcilaso explains,

> has three meanings: exchange, give, and take, and it was a very suitable name for these men since they exchanged, received and gave messages, from post to post. The messages transmitted in this manner were always oral, for the reason that the Incas had no written language. They were composed, therefore, of a few simple precise words, in order that the messengers should not risk changing their meaning or forgetting some of them.

Chasquis' messages were also top secret. A number of conquistadors complained that, however hard they tried to get a *chasqui* to tell them what his message was, they never got an answer, even in the face of torture and death.

In addition to their oral messages, *chasquis* also frequently relayed a *quipu*, the unique statistical tool that made Inca administration possible.

The *quipu* was an abacus on strings. It worked on a decimal system, with knots representing the numbers and a space between the knots standing for zero. A *quipu* usually had one main string, representing the most important statistics to be conveyed, with an array of subsidiary strings, of different colors, representing specific

Moche messengers, like the ones on this vessel, carried incised beans to help them remember the contents of their message.
THE METROPOLITAN MUSEUM OF ART, GIFT OF NATHAN CUMMINGS, 1967

Inca messengers knotted the content of their news into a quipu, *a kind of abacus on strings, shown in this illustration.*
COURTESY OF THE AMERICAN MUSEUM OF
NATURAL HISTORY

categories of accounts. Thus, a main string might have knotted into it the number of taxpayers in a province, with the sub-strings containing the statistics on males and females in their varying age groups, the number of fields being cultivated, the size of herds, or the quantities of specific products.

KINGDOM OF THE SUN

Using *quipus*, with detailed information coming up all the way from the foreman in charge of fifty *purics*, the Incas conducted a complete census once a year. It was probably more accurate than the most sophisticated, computerized economic statistics we have today.

As Garcilaso puts it:

> Every year, an inventory of all the Inca's possessions was made. Nor was there a single birth or death, a single departure or return of a soldier in all the empire that was not noted on the *quipus*. And indeed it may be said that everything that could be counted was counted in this way.

Quipus were prepared by specialists called *quipucamayus*. Their number varied with the size of the community to which they were assigned, but even the smallest *ayllu* had at least four of these statistician-accountants. As usual in the Inca system, some were "inspectors," that is, they double-checked the work of their colleagues. Apparently, every *quipu* reckoning was checked at least three times to eliminate error as well as corruption.

Garcilaso claims that *quipus* even kept records of "battles, diplomatic missions, and royal speeches." But since accounts of such events are not a statistical matter, he says the *quipucamayus* collaborated in setting down these records with *amautas*, the teacher-historians who taught the princes, and with *harauecus*, poets, who, like Homer, the bards, or the minstrels, put the glorious deeds, brilliant thoughts or passionate encounters of their compatriots into cadenced rhythms.

VIII THE SPLENDOR OF LIFE

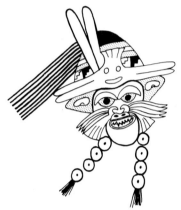

This is how Inca rhythms sounded: They come, not from a story but from a prayer, addressed to Pachacuti, the creator of the universe, who was also called Viracocha.

Viracocha, Lord of the Universe!
Whether male or female
At any rate commander of warmth and generation;
One who, even with his spittle can work magic,
Where are you?
Would that you were not hidden from this son of
　　yours.

He may be above, he may be below,
Or perchance abroad in space.
Where is His mighty judgment seat?
Hear me!
He may be spread among the upper waters,

Or among the lower waters and their sand
He may dwell.
Creator of the world, Creator of man,
Great among my ancestors,
Before my eyes fail me
I long to see you.
For seeing You, knowing You
Learning from You, understanding You
I shall be seen by You and You will know me.

The Sun—the Moon; The Day—the Night; Summer
   —Winter:
Not in vain, in orderly succession,
Do they march to their destined place, to their goal.
They arrive wherever You bear your royal staff.
Oh harken to me, listen to me,
Let it not befall that I grow weary
And die.

This prayer-poem survived the Spanish conquest. It has been handed down orally to the present day. An expert Peruvianist, the American anthropologist, Philip Ainsworth Means, translated it from the Quechua. It is characteristic of the Incas both in content and style. It bears witness to their deeply ingrained sense of order and obedience. It has no humor, no wit, no gaiety. Its tone is grave, almost melancholic, and its rhythms are even, carefully structured, sounding much like a footfall behind a plough.

All of the Inca arts were like that. While sometimes passionate, the passions expressed were usually those of loss or grief. There was tenderness, but little spontaneity, creativity or inspiration. In the realm of the Inca, the arts were fitted into a groove, designed to serve a planned purpose. Today we would call this style socialist realism. For the Incas the splendor of life derived from being part of what they were taught to believe was a splendid society.

Drama was perhaps the most characteristic of the Inca arts in illustrating how very precisely art was fitted into the social hierarchy, how unswervingly realistic it had to be, and how it served the political purposes of the state.

Garcilaso describes it succinctly:

> The *amautas* were quite clever at composing tragedies and comedies that were played before the king and the lords of his court, on high feast days. The actors were not yokels, but Incas or nobles, *curacas*, captains, and even camp commanders: each one, in fact, being obliged to possess in real life the quality, or occupy the function, of the role he interpreted. The themes of the tragedies were always taken from history, and usually related the triumphs and valorous acts of one of the early kings, or some other hero of the empire. As for the comedies, they treated of rustic or family life. When the performance was over each one returned to the position that was his, according to his station or occupation. The interludes too, were never unseemly, cheap or base, all, on the contrary, treated of subjects that were extremely serious, moral and sententious.

What theater was for the upper echelons of the social hierarchy, dance was for the lower. Dances were designed for specific occasions, and served a definite social purpose, having to do with either production or ritual. There was a seed dance, an irrigation dance, a hunt dance. For ritual purposes, there was a snake dance, a heron dance, a rope dance. The rope dance was a kind of pledging of allegiance in dance form. In Cuzco, the rope used was a golden one, representing the skein of Inca authority through the generations. Dancers approached it with slow grave steps, bowed to it deeply, touched it reverently. All dance steps were predetermined, like a ballet.

The music accompanying dances was a muted but martial counterpoint of flutes, pipes and drums. Garcilaso says that the Incas had a panpipe, made of reeds or clay that had graded tones, corresponding to the human voices of soprano, contralto, tenor and bass. In Peru and Bolivia, highland Indians play panpipes to this day, and the tunes they coax from these instruments are still grave and melancholic, with a deep and tender cadenced beat.

If drama and dance were the most characteristic of Inca arts, architecture was undoubtedly the most impressive. But it was impressive for its quantity and skill rather than its beauty or grace. The Kingdom of the Sun was studded with palaces, temples, storehouses and fortresses—many of which survive—in the unmistakable Inca style. The buildings were massive and built to last. They had the Inca architectural "signature" as unique as the "key" of the Greeks or the soaring arches of Gothic cathedrals. The Inca signature was a trapezoid niche, an opening cut into the wall, to serve either as a shelf for a piece of golden sculpture in a temple

The Inca were not great artists. The most exquisite work in the Inca empire was done by the coastal people, based on the artistic traditions of precursor civilizations. Thus, the expressive silver figurine is the work of the Chimu; the elaborate, painted ceramic jug is Mochica.

or palace, or as a storage place for household implements in the house of a *puric*. Sometimes, the niche was cut through the wall all the way to become a window.

Another characteristic of Inca architecture was the precision of its stonework. Like the Egyptians before them, the Incas had learned to quarry stone, to transport and erect enormous blocks of rock. The Incas used the stone in its natural form, only paring the edges to make them straight. Then they fitted the stones together, without mortar and so precisely that it is sometimes impossible to insert even a razor blade into the fittings. A famous example of Inca precision in rock masonry is the fortress of Cuzco, known as Sacsahuaman, which looms over the city, mammoth and commanding, much as it must have done when the empire was at the height of its power. The fortress has in its walls one large stone with twelve different angles, each angle fitted to another rock so closely and neatly that they look as if they had grown together, like petals in a flower of stone.

Victor von Hagen, the explorer who surveyed the length and breadth of Inca roads and has an explanation for almost every other Inca achievement, is as baffled as everyone else by this feat.

"How the Inca mason obtained this minute precision," he says, "in which the enormous stone had to be lifted and set down a hundred times before it fitted perfectly on all its sides like a bottle stopper, still cannot be satisfactorily explained."

The Spaniards, too, were impressed. Pizarro's secretary, Pedro Sancho, not one to give the Incas credit for anything if he could help it, writes: "The most beautiful thing which can be seen in the edifices of that land are the walls. They are of stones so large that anyone who sees them would not say that they have been put in

The Inca were, however, powerful architects. Their masonry was impressive; no one understands as yet just how they quarried, transported, and fitted the great stones that produced edifices like the fortress of Sacsahuaman, shown here, or "the bath of the Inca," just outside Cuzco, in the facing page.

PHOTOGRAPHS BY NOEL WERRETT

place by human hands, for they are as large as chunks of mountains and huge rocks."

While we do not know what special skill went into erecting these walls, we do know how the Incas planned their buildings and their cities. They worked from clay models and their urban planning was superb. Every town was carefully designed to incorporate into its architectural layout all the activities that were vital to an Inca metropolis. Once having arrived at a basic pattern, it was used throughout the realm. Anyone with an orderly mind could not possibly get lost in an Inca city—any Inca city.

Garcilaso says he saw an architectural model of Cuzco and the surrounding country. It was made, he reports, of clay, small stones and little sticks.

> It was constructed to scale, showing both the large and small open spaces of Cuzco, both its principal and less important streets, its different districts, its suburbs and all its houses, down to the very humblest, its three brooks and the starting points of the four great highways that cross the empire; it was really a pleasure to look at it. All the neighboring countryside was also marvelously reproduced, with its hills and mountains, its plains and valleys, its rivers and streams, including all their bends; indeed, the best cosmographer in the world could not have done better.

While the Incas were impressive and certainly prolific builders, they produced little that was notable in either sculpture or painting.

Inca architecture survives unscathed. This is an alley in Cuzco today.
JUDITH WHIPPLE

Inca ceramics did not have the flair and color of the work of the coastal civilizations, but was workmanlike and interesting, like this three-animals bowl.
PHOTOGRAPH BY CHARLES UHT. COURTESY OF
THE MUSEUM OF PRIMITIVE ART, NEW YORK

And the Inca loved the painted cotton hangings of the Chimu.
PHOTOGRAPH BY CHARLES UHT. COURTESY OF
THE MUSEUM OF PRIMITIVE ART, NEW YORK

The only Inca sculpture we know were those golden gardens of Inca palaces, convents of Chosen Women, and Temples of the Sun in which nature was faithfully reproduced in gleaming metal. Painting seems to have been confined to occasional designs over a doorway and to Inca ceramics, especially jugs and beakers, which were sometimes decorated with painted figures, usually of animals. The Incas also produced some painted textiles, but those, too, tended to be simple, realistic designs, representing the craft of applying pigment to cloth rather than painting as a creative art.

Inevitably, given their approach to life, the Incas were better craftsmen than artists. Their ceramics—for practical or ritual use—were simple but elegant in design and well-made. Their ornaments, usually fashioned of gold, but sometimes also of silver, copper, bone or wood, were precisely crafted, impressive at times for their size and the skill of their workmanship, but never inspiring.

The one exception to the skillful monotony of Inca art was fashion. It was not splendid like that of the Maya, or magnificent like that of the Aztec, but it could be very handsome indeed. The Incas had, after all, inherited and adapted the superb sophistication of the Paracas in the making of textiles.

Using the wool of llamas, alpacas, vicuñas and the guanaco, and cotton from the coast, the Incas spun yarns with delicate spindles of wood and thorn, wove cloth with elaborate twining, looping and coiling. They could make gauzelike fabric ranging from laces to fishnet, raised fabrics from tapestry to brocade, double-woven cloth, twill lace, voile, and knotted fabrics. They embroidered textiles, painted them, decorated them with featherwork. They tie-

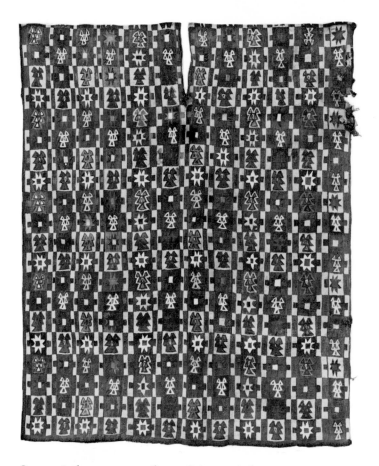

Some of the great textile traditions of the coast survived, as in this tapestry shirt of the Inca era.
THE METROPOLITAN MUSEUM OF ART, GIFT OF
GEORGE D. PRATT, 1933

dyed some fabrics, and copied from the Paracas most of their dyeing techniques resulting in the production of close to two hundred different hues. For their more elaborate creations, they apparently worked from samples, the fashion equivalent of the clay models from which they constructed their cities.

Handsome textiles were not confined to the nobility. While the reigning Inca and the higher nobility had their clothes made of the finest vicuña wool, and everyone else used cotton or the coarser

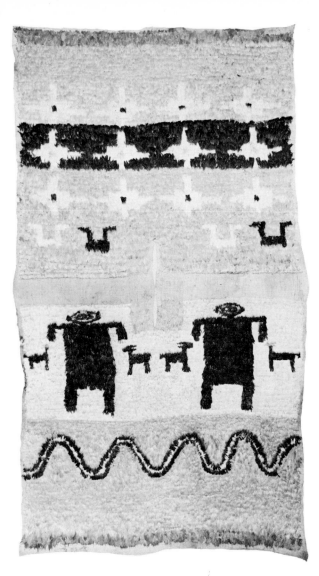

Another version of an Inca shirt, obviously meant for holiday wear. This one is made of cotton, with the decoration composed of feathers.
PHOTOGRAPH BY CHARLES UHT. COURTESY OF THE MUSEUM OF PRIMITIVE ART, NEW YORK

fibers of the llama, alpaca and guanaco, tunics and mantles, sashes and shawls, pouches and headbands could be elaborately woven and richly embroidered. Inca soldiers, for example, when not engaged in combat, wore a dress tunic of deep red, with a chessboard patterned border of black and white, the neck opening decorated with little golden pearls. Even the average *puric* and his wife could be fashion plates of a kind when they donned their second set of clothes, their "Sunday best" for special occasions.

The Incas invented the shoulder bag and both men and women used it. (Top)

The Inca knew lace, and sometimes used it as a headcloth. (Bottom)

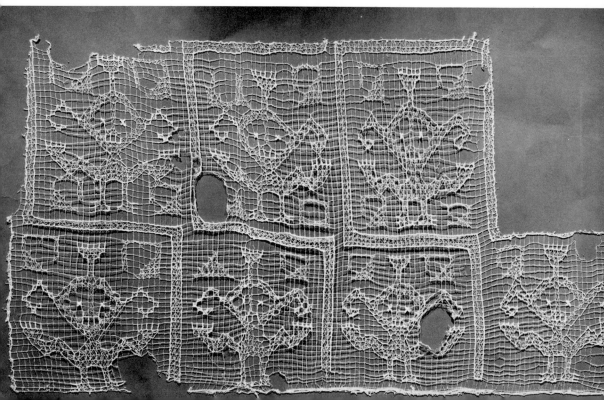

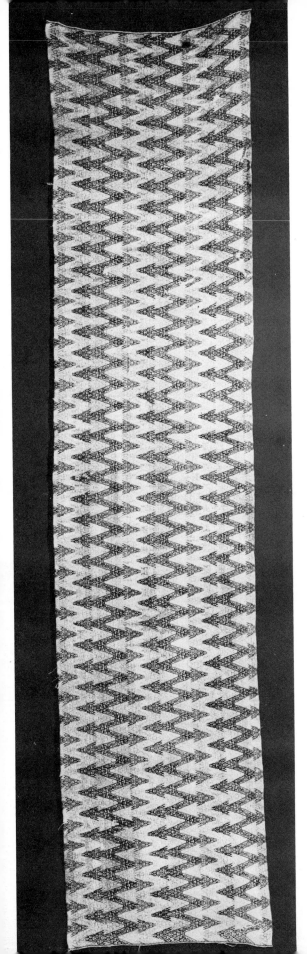

For their more elaborate textile creations,
the coastal people worked from a sampler,
like this one. (Top)
PHOTOGRAPH BY CHARLES UHT.
COURTESY OF THE MUSEUM OF
PRIMITIVE ART, NEW YORK

Cotton or wool girdles were often woven
in interesting patterns. (Left)
PHOTOGRAPH BY CHARLES UHT.
COURTESY OF THE MUSEUM OF
PRIMITIVE ART, NEW YORK

Some sashes got quite elaborate, combining
embroidery, appliqué, and a fringe. (Bottom)
PHOTOGRAPH BY CHARLES UHT.
COURTESY OF THE MUSEUM OF
PRIMITIVE ART, NEW YORK

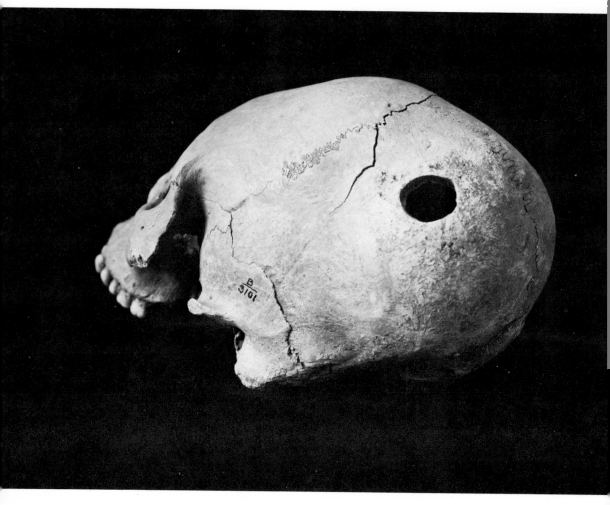

The Inca excelled at a special type of surgery called trepanning, which requires the surgeon to literally make holes in the head of his patient. The operation had medical and neurological reasons.
COURTESY OF THE AMERICAN MUSEUM OF
NATURAL HISTORY

One other art at which the Incas excelled involved special occasions of a different kind. It was a medical art, a special branch of surgery known as trepanning. Trepanning is skull surgery, in which holes are cut into the top of the head, primarily to relieve pressure on the brain caused by injuries. Since criminals were frequently punished by being beaten over the head with a club—the Inca equivalent to the lashes administered in punishment by their European contemporaries—they often became patients for trepanning. More numerous still were soldier patients. The main Inca weapon for close-in fighting was the cudgel, a mace consisting of a wooden handle with a fist-sized, star-shaped top of stone or metal. Soldiers hit each other over the head with this, and the injuries that resulted, if they did not lead to death, usually required the attentions of a surgeon adept at trepanning. There is also some evidence that melancholy in its more advanced state was relieved by the trepanning technique.

Given the state of medicine at the time, trepanning was undoubtedly more of an art than a science. The surgeons used finely edged, rounded blades as scalpels and seem to have been able to cut holes in a number of shapes: square and round, oblong and oval. There was, presumably, a reason for each shape, either medical or ritual. And there appear to have been a considerable number of subjects of the Kingdom of the Sun who, owing to one cause or another, walked around with holes in their heads. One source claims their number ran into the millions.

IX HISTORIC ENCOUNTER

Despite the meticulous statistics compiled by the Incas, accurate figures for the empire are hard to come by. There are two main reasons for this. For one thing, the Incas themselves had no written language. With the aid of the *quipu*, they managed to keep superbly well informed on current affairs, but they were in no position to keep permanent records. The Spaniards, for their part, were lackadaisical administrators, and the only item that really interested them enough to keep records on was gold. There are, therefore, fabulous figures on the amount of gold the conquistadors managed to lay their hands on in Peru, including the amounts they shipped to Spain. But there are no figures in Spanish records on products grown or animals raised; nor are there any figures on people.

Estimates of the population of the Inca empire when the Spaniards encountered it therefore range widely from as few as eight million to as many as thirty million. Thirty million would have been a staggering number for that time and place, far more than the Roman empire had at its height. The consensus seems to hover around ten million, which is roughly what the Indian population is today in the lands that belonged to the Inca empire.

Of one figure we are sure. In 1796, after some two hundred and fifty years of Spanish rule, the population of the Kingdom of the Sun had been decimated to a mere seven hundred thousand persons. This pathetic figure represents the blackest aspect of an historic encounter between two brilliant civilizations that met and clashed, with reverberations echoing down the centuries and causing political rumblings to this day.

The encounter began in the minds of two men. One was Francisco Pizarro, conquistador par excellence, whose career started as a swineherd in the south of Spain, but whose ambition, courage and inspiring leadership resulted in his becoming the conqueror of the richest domain known to the Europe of his day. The other man was Atahuallpa, the favorite son born to the eleventh scion of the Inca dynasty, Huayna Capac, and his Quito spouse. In Atahuallpa's mind there lodged a legend, widespread among all the major pre-Columbian civilizations, that there had once been a hero-god who came to teach important arts of life to the people of the hemisphere. One day he walked away eastward across the waters, promising that he would return someday, arriving again from the sea. The prevalence of this myth has led to the fascinating speculation that perhaps the Vikings, or some other European seafarers, had come to the Americas centuries before Columbus, had taught the Indian populations new skills, and had left again on their long boats. The Maya as well as the Aztecs had the same myth, with only the name of the hero-god varying. All the legends concurred that the hero-god was fair-skinned and bearded. When Atahuallpa encountered Pizarro, who was both bearded and comparatively fair-skinned, a mixture of deep-seated doubt and hope must have haunted the Inca prince.

The two men first set eyes on each other in November of 1532, in the highland city of Cajamarca, which still exists in Peru. Pizarro had landed earlier that year at the port city of Tumbes, in northern Peru, with two hundred cavalry men and foot soldiers. It was Pizarro's third try at finding the fabulous golden kingdom, rumors of which had floated north to Panama, then already under Spanish jurisdiction. These dreams of *El Dorado* haunted many a gold-thirsty conquistador and his receptive monarch in Castile. The Spaniards under Pizarro's command had slogged through the desert, climbed and clawed their way up the Andes to Cajamarca.

At the hot baths just outside the city, Atahuallpa was taking his ease after five years of intrigue and battle with his half-brother, Huascar, both claiming title to the kingdom. Their father, Huayna Capac, had died intestate and deeply divided between his affection for Quito and Atahuallpa and his obligations to Cuzco and Huascar. Solving the problem for himself, he left word that on his death he wanted his body cut up, his heart and liver buried in Quito, the remainder conveyed to Cuzco to be interned with his Inca ancestors. The tragedy resulting from this conflict of loyalties was that the empire soon found itself similarly cut up and divided.

Before his death, Huayna Capac had been told what would happen. A diviner, reading omens from a llama lung at the Inca's request, warned Huayna Capac: "The moon, your mother, tells you that Pachacuti, the creator and giver of life, threatens your family, your realm, your subjects. Your sons will wage cruel war, those of royal blood will die, and the empire will disappear."

The diviner was executed for his dire predictions, but his forecast turned out to be accurate nevertheless. When Pizarro and Atahuallpa met at Cajamarca, Atahuallpa and Huascar had been battling each other for the succession in wars that had indeed become increasingly cruel, ruthless and destructive. Historic happenstance found the Inca empire at its most fragile when Pizarro and his men undertook their own hazardous journey to the heart of the Kingdom of the Sun.

It is horrendous to contemplate the fact that the shattering of the Empire of the Sun took exactly thirty-three minutes. Such was the duration of the battle between the Spaniards, dug in at Cajamarca, and Atahuallpa and his retinue, who had come to the town at Pizarro's plea. They had come unarmed.

An eyewitness, Pizarro's Indian interpreter, Felipillo, whose nickname was Linguilla—Little Tongue—reports: "Atahuallpa was accompanied by five thousand. Three hundred swept the road before him; there were singers, dancers, and court officials. Atahuallpa was carried on a litter with a golden canopy of tapestry sparkling with precious stones."

Within minutes, a Spanish attack with horses and muskets had scattered the unprepared and deeply frightened retinue. The litter was overturned and, for the first time in the history of the Incas, a reigning son of the sun found himself on foot, alone, staring into the eyes of his enemies.

The Spaniards imprisoned Atahuallpa and, after asking for a chamber full of gold for ransom—and getting it—executed him anyway. There is interesting speculation on why Pizarro decided to kill Atahuallpa, since the two men apparently respected each other greatly and, during the months that passed between the first encounter at Cajamarca and the garroting of the Inca, saw each other daily and had developed a curious intimacy. The obvious political reason is that the Spaniards felt—and a number of conquistadors are on record as arguing this point—that as long as the Inca was alive his subjects would never accept Spanish rule. (Atahuallpa had earlier defeated and imprisoned the legitimate heir to the Inca throne, his half-brother, Huascar, and in a political gambit that finally proved to be Atahuallpa's own death warrant, had his brother killed.) Pizarro seems to have wavered on the point of Atahuallpa's execution, feeling that he could control Atahuallpa and use him as a puppet ruler, thus saving Spain, himself and his men a great deal of time and trouble. Linguilla, a native orphan who had attached himself to Pizarro when he was thirteen, says the real reason was different. According to Linguilla, Atahuallpa had discovered that Pizarro, alone among his fellow conquistadors, could not read. Pizarro knew Atahuallpa had uncovered this shameful secret, and the embarrassment induced him to agree to Atahuallpa's death.

Linguilla's story of how Atahuallpa discovered Pizarro's illiteracy sheds a fascinating light on the Inca's subtle intelligence. The Inca prince had asked one of his conquistador guards to inscribe the name of the Christian god on his fingernail and, as the guards changed, Atahuallpa asked each one to read the divine name. All of the conquistadors complied except Pizarro, who couldn't, because he had never learned to read or write. Pizarro assessed and finessed the problem when he was faced with it—as he had so many others in his spectacular career—but it seems the two men's eyes met and both understood. The encounter subtly changed the relationship between them. Pizarro no longer felt secure enough to let Atahuallpa live.

With their own strange sense of gallantry, the Spaniards made a solemn ceremony of Atahuallpa's execution. All the conquistadors attended it, dressed in deep mourning. That was in August, 1533. Ten weeks later, the Spaniards were in golden Cuzco, which they proceeded to strip quickly and methodically of all its precious metal. The imprisonment of Atahuallpa had been the beginning of the Spaniard's conquest of the Inca realm; the capture of Cuzco was its end. It led to three centuries of unmitigated plunder from which the countries of the Inca realm, and its peoples, have not yet recovered.

Such are the bare historic facts. Behind them, beneath them, and surrounding them was a clash of values and assumptions that made possible what would otherwise seem improbable and absurd. Atahuallpa accepted Pizarro's invitation to come to Cajamarca—Pizarro had requested that Atahuallpa dine with him—out of the oblivious generosity of an unquestioned ruler deciding to be hospitable to strange, even if unbidden, guests. The idea that there might be cause for caution never entered Atahuallpa's mind. He could not conceive of anyone laying hands on an Inca. Fear was a word that did not, could not, exist in his vocabulary. To the Spaniards, on the other hand, Atahuallpa was just another prince whose country they intended to annex to the crown of Castile by whatever means seemed most efficient. They had no scruples about him as a person, nor, of course, did they appreciate his presumed divinity. They had saints of their own. The conquistadors' special protector was St. James, *Santiago* in Spanish, and it was with their famous cry of "Santiago and at them" that the conquistadors charged Atahuallpa as he was carried by his retinue into the central plaza of Cajamarca.

The Inca and the conquistadors also had different notions of diplomacy. To the Incas, diplomacy was the use of reason and persuasion to make others agree to their political will. Inca diplomacy consisted essentially of telling the truth about the advantages that would accrue to anyone submitting himself to the Inca's will. The Spaniards had much the same aim, but a very different method. Truth, to the conquistadors, was a highly expendable commodity. They thought nothing of making up stories that fitted their purpose; of offering pledges and promises which they broke as soon as it suited them to do so, sometimes with intricate rationalizations for themselves and others, but also frequently by just changing their minds because it was more profitable to do so. The Incas soon became contemptuous of what they called the Spaniards' "honeyed words." To this day, the descendants of the Incas react with distrust and distaste to any pledge given, or any promise made, by a white man.

Warfare, too, was one thing to the Incas, another to the Spaniards. The Incas regarded warfare in the classical sense, as an extension of diplomacy: a policy to be applied after peaceful efforts have failed. The Spaniards tended to look at the relationship of warfare and diplomacy the other way round. Whenever possible, and sometimes when it seemed impossible, their instinct was to fight first and talk later. They were superb fighters: brave, skilled, and above all inventive, in both tactics and strategy. Surprise, always an important element in warfare, was the keystone of the conquistadors' battle designs. It had to be. They were usually outnumbered in proportions that still seem incredible.

The Spaniards also kept a sharp and wily eye out for the military weakness of their opponents. After encountering the Inca army on a number of occasions while fighting their way from Cajamarca to Cuzco, the conquistadors caught on to the rhythm of the Inca military machine: twenty days of fighting, ten days of rest. They therefore invariably attacked during the rest period, when the Inca army was in its most relaxed state. The Spaniards also discovered that the Incas never fought at night. Night battles quickly became the Spaniards' favorite tactic.

The major mistake the Incas made was their inability to conceive of reinforcements reaching the Spaniards by sea. Being essentially a highland people, the Inca thought of the sea as a frontier. Everything ended at the water's edge. They had heard of the legendary god-hero walking away across the water. They could somehow conceive of a mythical personality returning that way. And they knew, of course, of their own divine ancestors rising out of Lake Titicaca. But to them this was the stuff of legend, not strategy. Their notion was that if they could drive the Spaniards west, into the sea, that would be the end of the conquistadors. It wasn't. It was, in fact, the source of Spanish supplies, both men and arms.

Disease was another important factor in weakening the Incas. Inca medicine was fairly advanced for its time and adequate for the purpose of keeping the population reasonably healthy and growing. This changed when the Spaniards came. The conquistadors brought European diseases, ranging from measles to smallpox, to which the Incas had built up no immunity. The Spaniards could suffer from such diseases and survive. The Incas died of them by the hundreds of thousands.

The two peoples had different attitudes even to the common fate of death. The Spaniards believed in the Christian immortal soul which, if a man had done as conscience and the clergy bade, would survive and find a resting place in heaven. The Incas believed that the spirit returned whence it had come, but in order for it to do so the body had to be preserved. Ruling Incas, at the time of death, were mummified and installed with great splendor in palace tombs, with wives and servants to attend them. They were served ceremonial meals for years. Warriors and *curacas* were entombed in stone towers, dressed in full regalia, the tools of their trade by their side. Even the average *puric* was reverently buried in the family *huaca*, a mound tended with care by each family and respected by the entire *ayllu*. The word *huaca* is a composite of two Quechua words, *hua ca*, I-from-which, meaning, in conjunction, whence I came.

When Atahuallpa was to be executed, he was told that he would be burned, as all heretics were in medieval Europe, unless he agreed to be baptized, in which case he could be garroted instead. Having earlier rejected all attempts at conversion with the very understandable arguments that he already had a god and needed no other; that he was himself a son of god and therefore had no cause to worship another son of god; and, finally, that he could make no sense of the trinity—three beings that are one—he finally agreed to baptism because he did not want his body to go up in flames. He wanted it to be buried with the bodies of his paternal ancestors in Cuzco. When he was executed, a number of the wives and servants who had come with him to Cajamarca, and remained to serve him during his incarceration, killed themselves so that they could accompany him in death. This horrified the Spaniards who saw in it a demonstration of Inca savagery. They had little objection, however, to slaughtering women, servants, or anyone else, when it suited their purpose.

Two stories, and the names of a street and a city square, illustrate the deep differences that underlay these two civilizations, which clashed with such devastating impact. The stories concern gold. To the Incas, gold was the sweat of the sun, to be regarded with tender, loving care and used only for ritual purposes: in temples, convents or Inca palaces.

To the Spaniards, gold represented wealth and power, to be amassed in as large a quantity as possible for practical, temporal use. One of the first acts of the conquistadors when they entered Cuzco was to strip the Temple of the Sun of its radiant symbol, the golden, sunlike disc that shone over the main altar. The conquistador who helped himself to this booty settled down to a night of gambling when his day's work was done. He had a run of bad luck and, pushed to the end of his resources, wagered his newly acquired golden disc, and lost it just before dawn. From this event comes a famous Peruvian saying: "to gamble away the sun before it has risen."

This particular sun apparently changed hands a number of times, winding up finally in the possession of the Duke of Toledo who sent it as a present to Philip II, then King of Spain. Philip, a devout Catholic, in turn presented it to the Pope. Thereafter it vanished, and to this day no one knows in what dark corner of a European storehouse the sun that shone over the high altar of *Coricancha* finally sank.

Another golden symbol of the days of the historic encounter has similarly vanished without a trace. At the birth of Huascar, elder brother of Atahuallpa, the priests of Cuzco ordered a golden chain made, to be used in the ritual rope dance that was traditional at the birth of a prince. The chain, of massive gold, was enormous, long enough to crisscross the main plaza of Cuzco. Bearers were carrying it to Cajamarca as part of the ransom for Atahuallpa, when they heard on the way that the Inca had been killed. Having received the tragic news, they hid the chain where the gold-profaning Spaniards could never find it. It is rumored to lie at the bottom of a secret, sacred lake, and some Indians allegedly still know where it is. But no one has been able to discover who these Indians are and no expedition—several have been organized—has yet been able to find the famous chain. Inevitably, there are rumors that the chain will reappear when an Inca prince again assumes the throne of the Kingdom of the Sun in Cuzco.

The famous main square of Cuzco, where the chain was first used to celebrate the birth of Huascar, was called, under the Inca, the Square of Joy. Under the Spaniards, the same square became known as the *Plaza de Armas*, Weapons' Square. The main street that led from the square to *Coricancha* temple, designated Street of the Sun under the Inca, became Prison Street after the Spanish conquest.

The Spaniards, who faced grim challenges and horrendous haz-
ards of their own in conquering Peru, did not have an easy time of
it either after the conquest was accomplished. The conquistadors
had no talent for orderly economic systems and no patience for
sound administration. Within a year after establishing their regime
in Cuzco, they had managed to ruin a smoothly functioning economy and so distort all economic values that in a country dripping
with gold they had succeeded in creating rampant inflation. A
contemporary of the conquest years reports that in Cuzco a casket
of wine went for the equivalent of $1,700 in gold; a pair of shoes
for $850; a horse for $7,000. Creditors, he says, hid from their
debtors because they did not want to get paid in worthless gold.

The conquistadors themselves, having stripped the country of
precious metal, discovered that their kind of greed became absurd
in the land of the Incas. No one, after all, could eat gold, or drink it,
or build a house with it. Inca *purics* or masons, any Indian from
whom the Spaniards wanted and needed goods and services, simply
had no use for gold. To them, it was still the sweat of the sun, an
object of worship, not an article of trade. The smarter of the conquistadors therefore took their rewards from the Spanish Crown
in the form of land grants. After the conquest, all land in the Inca
realm was considered property of the Spanish Crown, which distributed it as it saw fit, in enormous parcels.

One experienced conquistador, Pedro de Alvarado, who had
been the main conqueror of the Maya in Guatemala a decade
earlier, decided after participating in the Peruvian conquest that
what he wanted for his pains was Quito, all of it. The Crown of
Castile did not think that a good idea, mainly because Alvarado

had an unpleasant reputation for ruthlessness which, while perhaps desirable in a conquistador, was not considered—even in Madrid—ideal for an administrator after conquest was accomplished. Alvarado was paid off instead with 120,000 pesos of gold, the equivalent of about $25 million in today's value. Since Alvarado already ruled the Maya of Guatemala as viceroy, he took the gold.

Another conquistador, however, Diego de Almagro, was unwilling to settle for the already debased metal. He asked for—and got—Chile instead, all the land stretching from what today is the border of Peru, south to the Maule River at about 35° latitude, which was the frontier of the Inca empire, marked by posts of gold.

Under this system, each of the soldiers who had landed at Tumbes and survived the conquest, ended up with gigantic landholdings, some of which have come down the family tree to this day.

The conquistadors were not only greedy beyond belief, economically inept, and administratively chaotic, they were also politically dissolute. Conquest was followed by years of rivalry and antagonism, sometimes degenerating into assassination and open warfare between individual conquistadors or groups of conquistadors banding together in opposing groups. They fought each other for land and power in Peru and for preference and perquisites at the faraway Court of Castile.

Pizarro himself was killed by some of his former comrades-in-arms in June of 1541.

A few years before his death, Pizarro married an Inca princess, the sister of Atahuallpa. However wrong-headed in their assumptions and narrow-minded in their religious and cultural values, the Spaniards had no prejudices of blood or race. Many conquistadors married Inca women, usually of the nobility. Their descendants— a handsome amalgam with creamy-copper skin and deep black hair, and eyes that have the molten chocolate hue of the classic Spaniard but tilt up unexpectedly at the corners—became the ruling families of Peru.

This personal fusion provided a satisfactory solution for a number of individuals, but for the overwhelming majority in the lands once governed by the Inca the basic problems—social, economic and political—that were created by the historic encounter between the Crown of Castile and the Kingdom of the Sun remain to this day.

X THE MAN IN THE MANTLE

What else remains? In the National Museum of Archeology in Lima, at the heart of that rich and rambling, many-halled institution, a tall glass case presides over the surroundings. It contains "the man in the mantle," a male figure with the coloring, features and bearing of an Inca, wearing an Inca headband and Inca sandals, and swathed shoulder to ankles in the folds of a mantle every inch of which is covered by exquisite embroidery. The mantle is in the style of Paracas, the Inca precursors on the coast whose famous textile arts were absorbed by the Kingdom of the Sun. The man in the mantle radiates all that was most glorious about the Incas: dignity deriving from discipline, pride based on accomplishment, security anchored in order.

In the highlands of Peru, much else survives as well. First, the people themselves, now as then comparatively short (about five feet) but stocky and well built, with strong, long muscles in their arms and legs and very broad chests. The chests contain particularly large lungs which the Andean peoples seem to have developed over the centuries or, more likely, millennia. These extraordinary lungs make it possible for the Andean highlanders to breathe, work, and live normally at heights of two to four miles. At such heights most human beings are quickly fatigued, and many become dizzy and faint because their bodies are not used to the shortage of oxygen at such altitudes.

Andean highlanders also have more red blood corpuscles than other members of the human species, designed to carry more efficiently through the body what little oxygen exists in the rarefied air. Their skin, basically brown, shading from light to medium, has a particular sheen of glowing red, something like a ripe, red apple. Their hair is glossy black. Eyes are brown with the fold at the corner that indicates their millennia-old ancestry in Asia.

Inca costume survives, with some changes. Trousers have taken the place of the breechclout for men, but the tunic-poncho is still worn, as is the shoulder bag and the knitted wool cap. Women's skirts are still long, but they are no longer made of one piece open at the neck. They start at the waist now, and tend to be voluminous. In some highland areas, where it gets freezing cold, the skirts are made of felt and women wear several layers of them, in bright primary colors: red, yellow, blue. Most of the women still wear the traditional stole that can double as a covering for the head. In some highland areas, however, women took a fancy to bowler hats— stiff, old-fashioned, round derbies, which they wear in all kinds of colors, tilted at a rakish angle over one brow.

Jewelry is as rare today for both men and women as it was in the imperial days. Now, as then, the only persons wearing personal

A Peruvian girl today. The hair is glossy black, the skin rose-brown, the eyes chocolate brown with the fold at the corner that indicates the Indians' Asian ancestry.

ANN MCGOVERN

*Inca ear spools, made of gold and silver. Inca nobles
wore heavy ear ornaments which distended their lobes.
As a result, the Spaniards referred to them as* orejones,
meaning "big ears."
PHOTOGRAPH BY CHARLES UHT. COURTESY OF
THE MUSEUM OF PRIMITIVE ART, NEW YORK

adornment are the *curacas*, today's administrators of Inca communities. One community with its own traditional administration
is Pisac, not far from Cuzco. Each Sunday the governing *curacas*,
dressed in costumes that seem to be a blend of Inca with Spanish
colonial, walk in solemn procession from the church to the market
to the community house, to inspect, arbitrate and judge, as in the
old days. Like the reigning Incas, they carry maces, and wear
earrings. Their faces, reddish brown and deeply etched, look as if
they were carved in leather, and their expressions are startlingly
similar to that of "the man in the mantle" in his glass case at the
museum in Lima.

As in most American lands conquered by Spain, the overwhelming majority of the population is now Catholic, at least nominally. There is little doubt, however, that the Indians of Peru still feel a particular intimacy with the stars and planets that play such an important part in the round of their life: the sun, the moon, the morning star. They also have a deep reverence for their ancestors and the *huacas* in which these forebears are interred.

Many of the skills and habits of imperial days survive as well in the Indians' personal lives and in their social relationships. The fields of the Peruvian highlands today look much as they did before the Spaniards came. Terraces—square, oblong, scalloped—climb the mountainsides, covered with green in the spring. Farmers use the same irrigation, the same fertilizer, and grow the same crops. The Incas reportedly grew 250 different kinds of potatoes and the variety of potatoes one can still see in a Peruvian highland market is amazing. As in Inca days, a portion of the potatoes is dehydrated into a powder and stored for the long days of winter, when the potato powder is mixed with root vegetables and an occasional piece of dried meat to be cooked up into a stew.

Housing has not changed very much either. The average Indian dwelling in the highlands is still a rude hut of stone or sun-baked clay, with a roof of straw and very little furniture inside. The hearth is still a construction of stone with holes at the top, and cooking and eating utensils are stashed in niches cut into the wall. Beds are still made of straw mats and llama wool blankets. The only important change is the occasional transistor radio nestling in one of the wall niches that in the old days used to hold a household god.

Indian housing in today's Peru has not changed much
from Inca days: a hut of stone or sun-baked clay with
a roof of straw and little furniture inside.
JUDITH WHIPPLE

A little Peruvian shepherdess with her llamas.
ANN MCGOVERN

Markets, too, still bear a great resemblance to trade transactions in the days of the empire. Some markets have grown large and gaudy, the range of goods is much wider than it used to be, and of course money is used nowadays most of the time. But there are still markets where Indian men and women sit silently behind mounds of merchandise which they barter against other goods, using a pair of finely calibrated scales, with not a word or a coin exchanged. The merchandise can be potatoes or *coca* leaves, spices, herbs, powdered limestone, hand-knit caps, pouches or headbands. The caps sometimes look like small fortresses, with four corners sticking up like turrets.

In many ways, the descendants of the Incas do not live as well as their ancestors did five hundred years ago. They cannot, as in the old days, count on being supplied with the basic necessities of food, clothes and shelter. There are no more storehouses of the Inca to take care of everyone in times of need.

In recent years, an interesting phenomenon has appeared. The Indians have constituted themselves into *mitmakona* again, moving not at the order of the Inca for political purposes, but on their own initiative for economic reasons. They move from the highlands to the coast, mostly to the big cities, and there they set up *ayllus*, communities in which every family has its own house and yard, but all work together for the collective good. The official designation for these latter-day *mitmakona* settlements is "new towns." In Lima, the government admits that these modern *ayllus* are the best-run neighborhoods of the city.

The astonishing historic fact is that in their hearts and minds the Incas never really accepted defeat. By one of those strange

Market day in Pisac, where trade is barter and the barter is silent.
JUDITH WHIPPLE

Young Peruvian women of the highlands, with their bowler hats, their ponchos, their many-layered felt skirts.
ANN MCGOVERN

spurts of the human imagination, this Inca refusal has become a symbol almost half a millennium after the conquest of the Kingdom of the Sun was presumably completed. The last Inca to rule, at conquistador indulgence, in fact as a puppet of Spain, was Tupac Amaru, grandson of Huayna Capac and nephew of Huascar. The court at Madrid respected hereditary monarchies and thought for some time that it could govern Peru through the Inca hierarchy by turning the Inca dynasty into loyal vassals of the Castilian Crown. Perhaps it could have. But the conquistadors on the spot had no such political concern. They wanted to exercise power directly, with no intermediaries and no restraints. Using a trumped up charge of treason, they executed Tupac Amaru in December, 1571. They beheaded him. With the strange ambivalence so typical of the conquistadors, they buried his body with full pomp and honors in the Cathedral of Cuzco but stuck his head on a spike which they displayed in the Square of Joy that had become the *Plaza de Armas*, as a warning to would-be resisters to their absolute rule. Their brutal, if customary, gesture went awry. Instead of being frightened or horrified, the Inca's subjects came at night to worship the head of their ruler. They must have found a means of doing something about preserving the head as well. Perhaps they embalmed it. They certainly decorated it, as had been the custom for any ruling Inca who had joined his ancestors. A conquistador by the name of Captain Baltasar de Ocampo, writing about the execution of Tupac Amaru and its consequences, says—and you can almost see him shake his head in bewilderment as he put quill to parchment—"The Indians came by night to worship the head of their Inca. . . . The head became each day more beautiful."

Two centuries later, another Tupac Amaru led the Incas in rebellion against Spanish rule. Tupac Amaru II—it is not known whether he was a direct descendant of Tupac Amaru I or whether he took the name as a symbol—headed a broadly based resistance movement against the Spaniards in 1780. Rebellion flared all over the lands that had once been Inca. It was finally quelled, but it lit the flame of revolution that led, in the decades following, to the independence of South America from Spain.

Today, new rebels are reaching for the old name as their symbol. The urban, mostly young, mostly white, guerillas based in Uruguay who call themselves Tupamaros derive this designation from a contraction of Tupac Amaru. They see Tupac Amaru I as a symbol of injustice perpetrated on a defenseless people, and Tupac Amaru II as a symbol of rebellion against oppression.

The real descendants of Tupac Amaru probably do not concur with the specific goals and methods of the Tupamaros. But they do agree that there has been more than enough injustice and oppression in their lives and that a change is overdue.

The question is what kind of a change. The Tupamaros advocate radical, Marxist change—violent and immediate. Their views now reach a substantial number of men and women in Inca lands, via those transistor radios in household niches in the highlands, or on more conventional counters and table tops in the new *ayllus* ringing the coastal cities. Both Russia and Cuba send regular broadcasts in Quechua, propagating the Tupamaros' views.

At the other end of the political spectrum are the conservative, traditional vested interests—including some of those leading families of mixed Inca and Spanish derivation—who like conditions the way they are and want no change of any kind. This seems neither desirable nor feasible in an age in which the real revolution is the revolution of expectations that has swept the world to reach even the remote highlands of Peru and their denizens steeped in centuries of obedience and acceptance.

Between the two extremes stretches a large middle ground of people—Indian, Spanish, and mixed—who feel that the time has come to choose and use the best of both civilizations that have left their imprint on this part of the world: the order and responsibility of the Incas; the individuality and ingenuity of Spain. They agree that the marriage between the conquistador Francisco Pizarro and the Inca princess who became his wife should finally be consummated in all its facets; not only personal and cultural, but political and economic as well.

These people believe that the historic encounter that began at Cajamarca can still be fashioned, not into a tragedy but a drama, with the clash resolved so that it becomes a catharsis for all the people of Peru and even, perhaps, an example for mankind of how two political and economic systems, seemingly opposite in their assumptions and structures, can, after all, learn to accept the best from each other and live together in peace.

PART TWO

XI PRINCE OF CHAN-CHAN

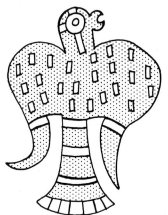

"Today, I will see the Inca. I, alone, face to face. Before this day is over I will have spoken to the emperor of the world. I will have looked into the eyes of the son of the sun."

Huaman's head spun at the thought. He had a sensation of floating, as if his whole being were bathed in a golden glow. As in fact it was. The sun had just come up in the east and its rays reached out for the narrow trapezoid doorway in which he stood, looking out over the golden city. The sun danced on the gold-flecked straw roofs, bounced back from the gold facings of the palaces and the Temple of the Sun. Holy Square, fronting the Temple, and the Square of Joy, where the festivals were held, looked like pools of gold. He lifted his arm to shield his eyes against the dazzle.

The movement made him feel as if he had wings. It would not have surprised him if he had found that he had grown wings overnight. After all, his name now was Huaman, falcon, and he felt as if the spirit of the soaring bird had indeed made its home inside him. His mind and heart felt light as a bird, his body lithe and powerful—like a falcon streaking across the skies.

He had earned the name Huaman during the thirty most grueling, most glorious days he had spent in the sixteen years of his life. He could still feel the strain of the effort in his muscles, taste the sweetness of the triumph from the edge of his teeth to the pit of his stomach. Staring straight at the face of the sun, he flexed his hands and ran his tongue over his lips. The sweet pain was still there.

It had all begun with a fast: six days of it, with nothing but water, a handful of greens each day and a very small bowl of cooked, unflavored corn gruel. During these days, he had slept on the stone floor of the barracks or on the bare ground in the barrack yard. Huaman had still not decided which of the two he disliked more. The stone floors had been harder, especially when the growling of his stomach kept him awake and, as the night crept by, he felt every bump and hollow of the stones against his aching body and itching skin. The plain earth had been softer; but it had also been colder out in the open, even at the very end of spring in these freezing highlands, and his blood was still not used to it. On the coast, where he was born, the sands were soft and warm and sleeping on the shore was pleasant the year round. He remembered too the moon on the coast, gentle and silver, not like the stars in these highland skies that had sparkled at him like the glittering points of lances.

A few of the boys had dropped out of the graduation exercises during the fast. Hunger induced some of them to withdraw; others collapsed under the rigors of the cold. Despite their four years of intense daily study, these boys would not be considered adults, would not be able to become either captains or *curacas*. Their families would feel disgraced. They would be, perhaps, unhappy for the rest of their lives.

Huaman shuddered at the thought. He had survived the six days without too much trouble, mainly by focusing his mind on the next period of the exercises, which was aimed at testing the young princes' skills and minds rather than their endurance. The passive virtues were not his favorite accomplishments—although he had learned to practice and appreciate them during his six years in Cuzco. What he really liked was active achievement, calling on all that was in him to reach a goal. And he loved the glory that rewarded this kind of effort.

He had had the chance to test himself to the limit. A meal after the long fast had restored their energies for the race from the exercise ground to the dark gray fortress that loomed over golden Cuzco like a gigantic shadow. It had been a long race, with stretches that plunged precipitously and laps leading steeply uphill. He had thought his lungs would burst when he finally reached the fortress gate. But he had been the first one to reach that gate and while tradition decreed that the winner's flag must go to the crown prince—who had arrived third—Huaman had received a small, stiff pennant of his own and his ears still rang with the shouts of *"haylli, haylli"* from the throats of the onlookers along the way.

In the war games that followed, he had also done very well. As the winner of the race, he had been given command of the squadron of princes quartered in the fortress, while another troop of graduates tried to dislodge them. Huaman's squadron had managed to defend itself and hold its position, but the next day, when roles were reversed, the princes under Huaman's command had also failed to dislodge the enemy. Huaman had thought of a strategy that might have worked: attacking stealthily at night. The princes had dismissed his plan disdainfully. Incas, Huaman had been told curtly, did not fight at night. They gave battle only when their father, the sun, could observe their valor.

In the exhibition sports that came next, no such differences of opinion arose. Huaman had performed beautifully, wrestling and jumping, fencing and shooting at targets with bows and arrows. On the coast, where he was born and had lived as a boy, Huaman had never seen a bow and arrow. The peoples from the other side of the highlands were the empire's experts at archery. But Huaman had learned that skill, too, and had done well at it during the graduation exercises. His best sport, however, was wrestling, where his nimble body movements worked to great advantage. The nimbleness, he had sometimes thought, came to him from having watched the fish of the sea. The highlanders tended to be stolid, to dig in their heels like a big animal, and just stand there, or lunge. You had to watch out for them when they were lunging. They had broad shoulders and big chests, and they packed a wallop that could crush your ribs if you did not get out of their way fast enough.

There had in fact been murmurs of discontent when Huaman had ducked to avoid some of the most powerful lunges during the bout. In the days following, when captains came at the graduates suddenly while the boys were standing guard and flashed switches across the graduates' arms and legs that stung and left mean welts,

Huaman had had to be very firm with himself to control his instinctive reactions. A prince was not supposed to cry out, or even flinch, as the rod came at him. Huaman could control his exclamation of pain, but it was difficult for him not to side-step the switch. It seemed such an easy and natural thing to do. But it would have meant failure at the exercise. The theory behind this seemingly perverse exercise had been explained to them in school:

"How will you be able to stand up to the blows of enemies wielding weapons if you cannot suffer the pain of a switch wielded by a man you know to be your friend?"

There was reason in that, Huaman thought, and the thought had sustained him during the onslaught of switches as well as during the even more distressing ordeal when a special inspector wielding a *macana*, a two-edged sword, strode among them and slashed about as if he were cutting corncobs from a stalk. Huaman had watched the swordsman practically gouge out one prince's eye, and the prince, a young member of the royal household, did not even blink. Noting this had given Huaman the fortitude to dig his own toes into the ground and never make a move when the swordsman swung at him low and seemed ready to split his ankles.

Among all the graduation exercises there had been one Huaman had really enjoyed. That was the graduates' time in the wilderness when they were sent out into mountains beyond Cuzco that they had never seen, with no food, no weapons, no shoes, and had to fend for themselves for a week. The task was to manage somehow to stay alive without raiding a village, and to come back to Cuzco not mauled by animals, without scratches or illnesses, looking like the princes they were. Those had been exciting days and nights, with every member of the team contributing ideas of how best to protect the group and take care of each other. The *awki*, Sinchi, son of the Inca Pachacuti's own sister, had been in Huaman's team and a sturdy, clever, dependable fellow he had proven to be. With Huaman and Sinchi leading, they had succeeded in keeping the entire team alive and well and looking like princes when they got back to Cuzco after the week was over. That, in fact, was how the young *awki* won his adult name, Sinchi. It meant leader.

Huaman's own name had been won in the same exercise. They had to hunt for some of their food and Huaman had proven expert at that. Sinchi had said so himself. Huaman had snared a wild vicuña that had provided the team with meat for three days. On the day before the last, when their stomachs had begun to growl again, Huaman had felled a falcon with a sling he had made from soft twigs and the wool of the vicuña, which he had wound round some tough highland grass so it had both power and resilience. Huaman had felled the falcon as it was swooping down on a little guinea pig. The little pig served as dinner that night, and the feathers of the falcon, black and glowing, clamped to the princes' hair, made the team's return to Cuzco not just an exercise satisfactorily completed but a triumph for all to see.

Huaman was very happy to have bagged that falcon. A prince had the right to be named after any animal he killed during the exercise, and Huaman would not have liked to be called vicuña. Vicuñas were fine animals and very useful. Their meat was delicate and their wool dressed Incas. But they looked fat and shaggy. And he was neither. Huaman—falcon—suited him much better.

He had really felt like a falcon in the glorious days that had followed the graduates' return to Cuzco, when all their efforts were rewarded and the strains dissolved in celebration. The Inca himself had addressed them and personally pierced the earlobe of each prince who had successfully completed the course. The Inca did this with a sharp golden pin that was left in the ear so that the hole would heal around the pin and be large enough to anchor the earring that was the mark of any man who mattered in the Kingdom of the Sun. The piercing must have been painful, but Huaman remembered nothing of that. His mind and body had been inured by then. What he did remember was the Inca's face: a face stamped by majesty and high seriousness. The Inca Pachacuti looked regal and wise. Except for the eyes. The eyes were set very deep and, it had seemed to Huaman, were filled with sadness.

But why would the son of the sun have eyes that looked like dark pools?

"I will ask my father when I see him later this morning," Huaman decided. "Or perhaps, if I dare, I will ask the Inca himself."

On the final day of graduation, Huaman had had no chance to say much to anyone. After the Inca himself had pierced his ear, he had been sent to another part of the sacred field, where the Inca's brother had given Huaman his first princely sandals, made not of leather thongs but of fine vicuña wool. The sandals had felt luxuriously soft on Huaman's feet, which had been worn raw by the barefoot days in the wild country.

In a third enclosure, another group of the Inca's own *ayllu* had been assembled and there Huaman's father had stood among the princes. In that enclosure, Huaman had been handed his arms: sword, lance, sling and battlestick.

Finally, there had been the ceremony at the indoor enclosure, the investiture that proclaimed him a man all through, when he was awarded his first breechclout of soft, white wool. He was wearing it now—he would never be without it for the rest of his life—and its white tassels showed just a little below his embroidered tunic. The breechclout, the soft sandals, the gold in his ears, and the *llautu's* wool ribbon wound several times round his forehead made it unmistakable to anyone who saw him today, and from here on, that he was a man, a prince in the Kingdom of the Sun.

Walking from his section of the town to the center of the city, Huaman was indeed treated differently than he had been before his graduation. Adults, men and women, greeted him respectfully, and some even stepped aside demonstratively to let him pass. A month earlier, before his investiture, when he had walked from school to his home in the northwest quarter of the city, no one had paid him much mind. He had been just another of the young foreigners whom this sophisticated metropolis, the navel of the world, absorbed with casual ease.

The process of adaptation had been less easy for Huaman. He had been ten years old when he first came to Cuzco from Chan-Chan, the lovely city on the coast where his father was the powerful king of the Chimú. When the king of the Chimú finally pledged his allegiance to the Inca—a pledge most graciously accepted by Pachacuti—part of that acceptance was an invitation for the king's son to come to the court of Cuzco for his education. The Chimú prince, Pachacuti noted, would be taught the Inca arts of peace and war, the imperial language, Quechua, and the imperial way of life. It would be important for him, the Chimú prince, to know all this when he returned finally to Chan-Chan to rule. Huaman's father had readily agreed to the Inca's suggestion. It made very good sense.

"But did his father really have a choice? Could he have refused?"

The question flashed across Huaman's mind but he dismissed it quickly. He was glad he had come.

He had not felt that way in the first two years after his arrival in Cuzco. The city had been exciting even then, but he had spent most of the time in the house of the representative of the empire's northwestern quarter, who was a very busy man. The *curaca* had had little time to pay attention to the young prince from Chan-Chan. The women of the household had been kind to Huaman, but he could hardly even communicate with them at first. They spoke only Quechua, and he, of course, knew only his native Yunga tongue. He had been lonely, bored and homesick.

All that had changed when he turned twelve and began to attend the academy for young princes of the empire. His schoolmates included members of the Inca's own *ayllu*—his friend Sinchi was one of those—as well as relatives of the Inca, with genealogies carefully kept over generations, along with young lords from the coast, from the highlands to the north and south, and even from places on the other side of the mountains. It had been fascinating to talk to all of them about their own homelands, their own people, their many different ways. What an exciting world it was, this Kingdom of the Sun, Huaman had thought many times in those four years. And how lucky he was to be part of it.

"Even luckier now," he mused, "when I will have a role of my own in it, will help to keep it great and glorious, perhaps even make it greater and more splendid still."

Huaman had heard rumors that the Inca Pachacuti was planning to push the frontiers of empire, marked by golden posts, further, in the north and in the south.

"That would be marvelous," Huaman thought. "And I would love to be part of the effort. Everyone is better off when they are absorbed in the realm of the sun and have the Inca look after their welfare."

Huaman had learned during his four years at school that this was so and why it was so. He had been taught how to survey territory—its natural features, as well as its populations—and to make relief maps so that the land and its uses, for peace or war, could be understood at a glance. This was a very useful piece of knowledge, he had thought, which his father, a great ruler in his own right, had never possessed.

Huaman had also been taught how rulers in the Inca empire kept accurately informed on everything the realm produced: people or produce; babies born to man or to llama; crops grown and animals raised on the coast, in the highlands, on the other side of the mountains. It was done with the aid of a *quipu*, an intricate system of strings and knots, which was also unknown in Chan-Chan. The Chimú had had experts of their own in recording and transmitting information—the bean readers who made marks on hard-shelled beans which they could reinterpret—but the bean readers' knowledge was confined to ideas, and their information was not nearly as accurate or dependable as the knowledge that could be recorded and transmitted on the *quipu*. The art of knotting a *quipu* accurately, so that it contained the full information, had puzzled Huaman a little and, truthfully, had made him impatient. As a prince he had no need to knot a *quipu* himself. But he had to be able to read it. And that he had mastered.

At the academy he had also learned to follow the movements of the sun and to plot its course so that he knew what the seasons would be each year, when they would begin and end. It was the priests' task to tell the people when to plant, sow and harvest and they did this using the same knowledge Huaman had been taught.

But it was wise for a ruler to know what his priests were doing and be able to check on their accuracy and performance. After all, the ruler had to make certain that everyone in the empire had the food, clothing and shelter they needed, and this depended heavily on crops and animals being attended to in their season.

The arts of war that Huaman had been taught at the academy were not new to him. The Chimú had been great warriors in their time, and still ruled a sizable stretch of coast containing many other peoples that had been incorporated into the Chimú kingdom by conquest. The Chimú had, in fact, fought the Incas themselves in battles so furious that even the sons of the sun remembered the clashes with respect. In the end the Chimú had lost and Huaman now understood why that had happened. Inca strategy was subtler: it included the use of diplomacy and political persuasion. And Inca tactics were more complex: they used feints and diversions, and attacks that encircled a foe from both sides because the Inca knew every aspect of the terrain. They got that precious knowledge by just looking at those marvelous relief maps of theirs. The discipline of the Inca army was better, too. Everyone who served the Inca could depend on being well fed and well clothed, and could be certain that his home and family were looked after in his absence. This had not been true in the kingdom of Chimú. Wives and children had to fend for themselves when their men were away at war, and Chimú families often became part of an enemy's booty. The Inca soldier had no such concerns and therefore could concentrate completely on battle. It was, Huaman concluded once again, an excellent system. He would most certainly introduce it in Chan-Chan when he succeeded his father.

His father: He would have a great many questions to ask him when he saw him later in the day. What, for instance, really happened when the Chimú fought the Inca and when they made peace? He had been small when all that happened—only eight—but even he remembered his proud father declaring in the great assembly court at Chan-Chan that he would never surrender his kingdom, never abandon his people to the sovereignty of an alien lord. Huaman even remembered his father's defiance of his own Chimú lords when these lords had been beaten in battle and had come to plead with their king to ask pardon from the Inca—who was known to be generous and wise—and join the Kingdom of the Sun.

It was true that his father had finally done just that: asked for pardon and received it, on terms that were indeed generous and wise. He ruled his kingdom still and his people were more prosperous and more secure. The Incas had extended and improved irrigation, had built storehouses, had extended roads all along the coast as well as the roads leading to the mountains from the valleys along the sea. The Incas built a big fortress at Paramonga that seemed to watch over the Chimú kingdom like a shepherd over his flock, exuding safety and serenity. And the famous *chasqui* messenger service now connected Chan-Chan with all the other big cities of the empire including, of course, Cuzco. These innovations had made it possible for Huaman's father to travel comfortably and quickly from Chan-Chan to Cuzco to attend the graduation. Father had looked resplendent, Huaman recalled proudly, in his turban and emeralds and his nose ring of gold, as he stood among the Inca princes. He had looked just as splendid during the festival days that had followed, the *Inti Raimi*. When the Inca had shared his golden cup of *chicha* with the most deserving of his subjects, however, Huaman's father had not been one of the chosen few *curacas* and captains who had been honored. And he had looked alien and somehow remote attending the festivities in the Square of Joy.

"What really did happen between my own people and the Inca?" Huaman wondered.

At school he had been taught that the great Chimú had asked to join the Kingdom of the Sun, having heard, like so many other great kingdoms, of the wisdom and virtue of Pachacuti and the glory and power of his realm. They had been received into the empire as vassals who now cordially obeyed their supreme ruler.

Huaman had liked the lessons in history, taught by special instructors who told their stories in rhythmic cadences that were pleasing to the ear and easy to remember, and presented to their pupils painted boards that illustrated major events. The lessons had been entertaining and interesting always, but Huaman wondered just how complete was the story they told. There had, for example, never been any mention of the battles fought by the Chimú, of their bravery, of their own power and glory before they joined the empire, or of his father's long hesitation.

There had been other history lessons that made Huaman wonder. The story of the Inca's origin, for example, of Manco Capac and Mama Ocla, the first of the Inca rulers, who rose out of Lake Titicaca at the behest of their father, the sun, to take command of the people of the world and teach them the arts of civilization.

Many of these arts had existed in the kingdom of Chimú before it ever heard of the Inca, Huaman reflected; and besides, all he had ever seen rise from the sea were fish, not people.

Huaman was so lost in his thoughts as he walked that he almost did not notice he had arrived at the part of the palace that contained the academy. Having made the trip every day for four years, his feet had just taken the familiar path. It was the last time they would do so, and the realization gave Huaman a pang of regret. He had gone to the academy this day because the chief of the *amautas*, the philosopher-teachers, had sent word that he wanted to see Huaman. Huaman had wondered just what the *amauta* wanted to see him about. The message had given no indication.

The first person he encountered at the school, however, was not the *amauta* but Sinchi, his Inca friend of four years, with whom he had so completely and happily shared the strenuous days in the mountains, when they had to live entirely by their wits. The two had found that their personalities and skills mixed and matched to perfection. Huaman's eyes lit up and the web of thoughts and questions he had spun in his head blew away at the sight of Sinchi. He hailed his friend. To Huaman's surprise, Sinchi returned his salute formally, sternly. His eyes met Huaman's but while for four years they had held messages which Huaman understood almost without words, they said nothing now. The look was hooded, opaque. And no words were proffered as Sinchi walked past Huaman and out of the school, to his home, the palace.

Huaman stood where Sinchi had walked past him, rooted to the spot. The school's courtyard was suffused with light, but Huaman felt as if he himself was suddenly wrapped in a shadow. It settled in his head, making his forehead and face feel dark and cold. It enveloped his body, leaving a vague distress, a kind of blueprint of sadness.

Huaman shook himself. Sinchi had probably just been preoccupied, the way he himself had been on his way to the school. After all, Sinchi too was an adult now, a full Inca, with a great many new tasks and responsibilities. They probably weighed on his mind.

The *amauta* coming toward Huaman must have read his mind.

"It is different now," the teacher said abruptly. "You must get used to it. Sinchi is a member of the royal *ayllu*. You, however brilliant and beloved, are a foreign prince. He is your superior. This will never change, and you must both act accordingly."

Huaman looked straight at the *amauta*. "I understand," he said. "But does this change the heart of our friendship, the way we feel about each other, have felt for many years?"

The *amauta* regarded him with a glance that seemed to burn itself into Huaman's mind. "Yes, it does," he pronounced, and his voice as he said it was solemn, the way it had always been when he recited history. "It must change. Duty and propriety demand it. It therefore cannot be otherwise."

Huaman nodded acknowledgment. As he did so, his head felt heavy as a rock.

The *amauta* had watched Huaman closely and seemed pleased by the response. His voice and tone reverted to their more natural, personal quality.

"Duty and propriety have their pleasing aspects also," he said. "Your brilliant performance at the graduation entitles you to some of them. I have been instructed to escort you this afternoon to the House of Chosen Women so you may meet one of the chosen whom the Inca will give you as wife when her own time of training is completed.

"I will call for you at your home and would like to use the opportunity to pay my respects to your father on his excellent son."

On the way back to his home, Huaman did not feel again the lightness of mind, heart and body with which he had greeted the day. Still, the *amauta's* compliment had been great and rare— *amautas* were not given to easy praise—and his father would be very pleased. And the thought of visiting a house of Chosen Women, and actually meeting one of them, made Huaman's stomach feel as if it had been invaded by some of those small flying fish he remembered seeing light up the waves on a moonlit night by the sea. During the *Inti Raimi* festival Huaman had seen some of the Chosen Women present to the Inca beautiful garments they had woven. He had watched other Chosen Women, Virgins of the Sun, dance in Holy Square, their long white robes clinging and billowing as they moved rhythmically in patterns of circles and squares. He had thought them beautiful and they had appeared in his dreams that night. To meet one of them was more than even that sweet dream had promised.

When Huaman told his father of the impending visit to the House of Chosen Women, he found, to his consternation, that the pleasure and anticipation he felt were his alone. His father was very proud of Huaman's performance at graduation, delighted by the *amauta's* compliment, and profoundly moved by his son's scheduled interview with the Inca. But the visit to the House of Chosen Women, and its reason, seemed to disturb him. Huaman decided that the cause of this disturbance was another topic on which he wanted to question his father, and that he might as well start their conversation by asking it.

"It is undoubtedly an honor," Huaman's father replied slowly, carefully, "to be given one of the Chosen Women as a wife. They are very well trained in all the domestic arts and make very good wives. But . . ." His voice trailed off as if he were unwilling to continue.

"But?" prompted Huaman.

The troubled look on his father's face deepened. "Their beliefs are as finely honed as their skills. Their faith in the sun is absolute and their devotion to the Inca as the son of the sun is complete."

"But I share this devotion and this faith."

"The devotion, yes. The Inca Pachacuti is a magnanimous and magnificent ruler. His policies are wise and just. I, personally, have learned from him the most important lesson of my life . . ."

Once again his father's voice trailed off in thought. Once again Huaman prodded him back to the present, to their talk.

"And what is that?"

"The first time I came to Cuzco, Pachacuti honored me by letting me walk in procession with the Incas of his own house and offered me the sacred drink from his golden goblet. No one heard his words to me because he kept his voice deliberately low as we drained our cups. But this is what he said, and I have never forgotten it:

" 'He who envies another injures himself.'

"It was true. My joy in the festivities had been marred by the question that haunted me then: why is his Cuzco not mine? Why does this glory belong to another prince? I have not asked myself that question since then and have been a happier man and a better ruler."

"Why then," Huaman asked, "should I not benefit from the same wisdom that enhances every aspect of a man's life as you yourself have said?"

Father nodded. "Indeed you should. In my journey to Cuzco to attend your graduation, I saw once again how much the Inca has done for all the peoples who have joined his realm. They are safe and content. But we, who can think and hope for more than safety and contentment, who remember achievements of our own, must go further. Perhaps we cannot help asking the question, at least in our own minds, of what is there in life beyond the daily round, beyond the rising and lying down to sleep, beyond the order that we know and the safety that we want."

Huaman blinked. He had not asked himself such questions as yet, except to wonder how two human beings could rise out of the water and be the children of the sun. But it had not seemed to matter very much because the sun was evidently such an important part of life, here, in these cold highlands. It provided warmth and made things grow. It had not been so in Chan-Chan. There, the sun beat down on the sand, on people and crops and, if it had not been for those deep aqueducts his father's people built many years ago, the sun would have shriveled and killed everything that grew. It sometimes did just that, when even the carefully collected and channeled water was not enough to keep the plants green with that merciless sun overhead. In Chan-Chan, the people worshipped the sea, which provided them with so many good things: fish and turtles and snails; grasses that grew at the shore; and, out on the islands, birds and the fertilizer these birds produced. In Chan-Chan no one believed there was a human being who was the son of the sun, or of the water either, for that matter.

Suddenly, Huaman remembered the temple at Chan-Chan. Worship there had not been very different from worship at Cuzco: sacrifices and divinations, songs and dances. The difference was inside the temple. In Chan-Chan, the Holy of Holies was not an altar with a glittering image of the sun, but a dark little chamber containing a small, frail, perishable figure of wood: an image of man, as, in fact, he was.

Father's voice cut into Huaman's memories. "I traveled to Pacha-camac on my journey this time," he said, "and visited the two temples there. The big temple that is dedicated to the lord of creation, who made everything but cannot be seen, only felt in the innermost core of one's being. I heard there that Pachacuti himself honors this creator and worships him in his heart.

"I also visited the second temple, the one that is dedicated to the oracle of Rimac, in which the Incas believe. They consulted the oracle before they attacked us and were told that they would win. In the Holy of Holies of the oracle, I found the same image that we have in Chan-Chan: man himself."

Once more Father's voice trailed off into meditation.

Huaman felt agitated. "Are you saying, then, that the sun is not the divine father, and the Inca not the son of the sun?" he demanded.

"Perhaps I should not burden you with such thoughts," Father replied. "You are young and must live your life in this Kingdom of the Sun. But indeed this is what I do believe. The sun is a powerful natural element and worthy of respect, as is the sea we know, as a giver of sustenance. Neither of them are gods. There is a creator who has made the sun and sea, the fish and the llama, the corn on its green stalk and the potato deep in the earth. That creator has also made you and me—and yes, the Inca himself.

"This does not mean that the Inca Pachacuti does not deserve your admiration and devotion. He is entitled to all you can give him. But it does perhaps mean that a Chosen Woman will not make the best wife for you, because she has no memories of other ways and no beliefs other than her faith in the sun. And that faith to her is as strong as life itself. She would consider blatant treason any doubts you may have, any questions you may raise, even in your own home."

Huaman felt his heart grow heavy. Not because of the things his father had said about the Chosen Women—Huaman remembered their dance and his dream, and those flying fish still leaped in his stomach at the thought of what the afternoon would bring— but memories suddenly crowded into his heart that were heavy, and sweet. He remembered how, when he was a very small boy, his father had taken him to hunt, all decked out in colorful breeches, wearing high leather sandals, his legs painted in gay colors. They had roamed the country with slings and arrows, look-ing for game, and had found the game down by the dunes of the sea or up in the green hills. These hunts had been free, wild and joyous. There had been a real contest between the hunters and their game, with the birds escaping many a time, and the animals running in unpredictable leaps and quite often getting away. When a hunter did bag his game, it was a personal achievement and left a feeling of triumph. And the hunters had come home happy.

Here in Cuzco hunts were not like that at all. There was just one hunt a year, organized by the Inca, and it involved no contest. Thousands of men, at the Inca's bidding, surrounded the animals of a region, driving them relentlessly into a circle where their fate was decided by fiat. The hunt was a chore, not a joy. And the hunters came home not happy, just tired from another day's work.

Other memories began to chase those of the hunt in Huaman's mind, memories going back further still to when he was a very little boy, three or four years old, walking about Chan-Chan with his nurse and a servant. How gay his companions had been on these walks, talking to each other and to him. In Cuzco, people were solemn, occupied and preoccupied. In Chan-Chan, his nurse had stopped to point out to him the gardens that dotted the city. Occasionally, they had walked through these gardens and she had broken off twigs of leaves and picked flowers to make a garland for his head. His hand reached involuntarily for his *llautu*. It was solid and significant, but suddenly, as he remembered those circlets of flowers, it felt scratchy and heavy on his head.

Huaman remembered, too, the nurse pointing out the sculptures on the walls of houses they passed: fish and birds, cormorants, pelicans and sea gulls, circles and squares in lovely, regular patterns. The fish seemed ready to leap, the birds poised to fly, and he remembered how his spirit had soared with them. In Chan-Chan, houses were painted inside, in many lively colors, so that it was a pleasure to step into anyone's home. Here, buildings were all stone and gold, and houses were somber inside.

Huaman looked at his father and a silence fell between them as sweet and heavy as Huaman's memories and as dark as the Cuzco chamber in which they sat. . . .

The excitement Huaman had felt earlier in the day trickled through him again when the *amauta* arrived to escort him to the House of the Chosen Women. It was not far, but they were going there in a litter, a conveyance Huaman had never been allowed to use before. Transport by litter was reserved for adult princes, governors and captains. Swaying regally down Cuzco's narrow, stone-paved streets, Huaman felt heady in three ways at once. The motion itself was rhythmic and, to one not used to it, it felt airy. Huaman also noticed the deeply respectful way people saluted the litter and quickly stepped aside to let it pass. If he had thought in the morning that walking through Cuzco with his breechclout and tunic, his pierced ears and distinguished *llautu* had created a stir, this ride on the litter doubled the respectful attention accompanying his progress through the city. It was a glorious ten minutes.

Sometime during the trip Huaman realized that the *amauta* himself was permitted to use a litter on this occasion only because he was accompanying an adult prince. During his four years at the academy, Huaman, like most of the other pupils, had occasionally deserved, and received, strokes on the soles of his feet, administered by the *amauta* with a birch, and the thought that the man who had administered these punishments was now facing him on a litter that he could command only because Huaman was with him, was a delightful morsel to savor during the ride.

Huaman did not let his face even hint at what was going on in his mind, but he was sorry when the litter-bearers stopped in front of the gold-sheathed walls of the House of the Chosen Women. He could happily have spent another hour being carried about Cuzco, collecting admiring glances and obeisant gestures; looking straight through the *amauta*, whom he now outranked; and gathering his thoughts and quieting his emotions about the unknown girl whom in his own mind he had already begun to call "my chosen woman."

She was not there when they entered the house. They were met instead—after having passed a forbidding row of guards and servants in an outer corridor—by an older woman, a *mamacuna*, who bade them a formal welcome and escorted them to the garden, which was quite unlike the sunken plots of flowers, grasses, and bushes that Huaman remembered from his walks as a child in Chan-Chan. This garden was made of gold. Golden llamas grazed among golden helms of grass; golden birds sat silent in golden boughs; a golden frog brooded beside the pool. Since there was no rustling of branches, no chirping of birds, no sounds of animals, the garden was completely silent. Eerily silent, Huaman thought, as if one had entered another world. The muscles of his stomach tightened.

The *mamacuna* had given him a quick, sharply appraising glance when they emerged into the light of the garden but was now addressing herself to his teacher, speaking very clearly and precisely, almost as if she were instructing the instructor.

"You understand," she said, "that Ima Sumac has only completed her second year of training. She must remain at least one more year in this house. During that year she must decide whether, on graduation, she wants to return to her family; marry this young man; or become a Virgin of the Sun and dedicate her life to the service of the sun and the sons of the sun. She has not yet made her decision."

The *amauta* inclined his head. "Yes, *mamacuna*, we understand. Will you please present the young lady."

Huaman sat rigid and silent—he hoped he looked cool and haughty—while the two elders exchanged conventions, gravely, with precise formality.

When Ima Sumac entered the garden a few moments later, his composure dissolved. He gasped, leaned forward to hide the improper sound, and almost dropped the present he had brought.

The name Ima Sumac, "How Beautiful," was exactly right. She was slender and graceful and moved like the tall water reeds Huaman remembered in the gardens of Chan-Chan. Her eyes, a very dark, brilliant brown, seemed to swim in small pools of white. Long, curving lashes covered them when she looked down. Her mouth was very full and pink, and reminded Huaman of a seashell. The face was oval, pale brown in color, with a red sheen on the high cheekbones. That sheen played games of light and hue with the blue-black glow that emanated from her long, thick hair. When she opened her mouth to bid them welcome, her voice, Huaman thought, sounded like the waves of the sea lapping against the sand on a summer night.

His hands moved as if they had a will and purpose of their own, to untie the feather-embroidered vicuña square in which his present was wrapped. His slim, tapered fingers, usually so agile and dexterous, caught in the knot of the cloth as he fumbled to untie it. He had never felt so clumsy. The package fell open at last to reveal a vase, beautifully shaped and exquisitely decorated with scenes of the sea: boats, fishermen, the long-necked birds and flying fish Huaman remembered so fondly and so well. Molded and glazed in the Chimú style, the vase was a deep black, with a silver sheen.

"It is the color of the sea, when the moon caresses it," Huaman stammered, holding out his gift to Ima Sumac.

She received it from him and cradled it in her hands. Her hands were so small and delicate that the vase looked like an enormous object. "The moon serves the sun," she replied.

What did she mean? Huaman wondered.

The *amauta* and the *mamacuna* looked approving.

The moon was supposed to be the wife of the sun. Was she saying that she wanted to be his wife when the time came, and knew this meant that it was her duty to serve him?

He wanted desperately for her to mean just that. "The moon is beautiful," he replied.

She inclined her head in agreement. "But the sun is glorious," she murmured.

Was she referring to him? To the relationship of man and wife? But she knew that he was not of the Inca's own *ayllu*, had no claim himself to being a son of the sun.

"Sun and moon each serve their purpose," he said carefully.

He had barely finished the sentence when he realized that he had said the wrong thing. The *amauta* looked embarrassed, the *mamacuna* disapproving. Ima Sumac's eyes flashed.

"There is nothing like the sun," she exclaimed, and her voice, so soft and lilting earlier, was husky, almost harsh, with passion. "The sun is supreme. Everyone in the empire knows that!"

The *amauta* asked leave to withdraw. The *mamacuna* nodded a quick assent. Ima Sumac, standing by the *mamacuna's* side, had lowered her lids so that the long lashes covered her eyes. She did not look up again as Huaman and his teacher left the garden.

Huaman and the *amauta* faced each other in silence as the litter made its way once more through Cuzco. Huaman wanted to ask just what Ima Sumac had meant by her remarks, and particularly by her last, passionate statement, but he did not dare. It was no longer proper for him to consult a teacher, and he was afraid of the answer he would receive. He knew in his heart what she had meant. It was treason to say that anyone or anything was equal to the sun, in any way at all, and only an ignorant foreigner could have even suggested such blasphemy.

In his mind, Huaman heard again the withering, almost contemptuous tone of Ima Sumac's voice when she said: "Everyone in the empire knows that!" He was certain now that to herself she had completed the sentence: "Everyone, except you." And he knew that Ima Sumac would never be his chosen woman. The flying fish that had leaped in his stomach only a short time ago had sunk to the bottom of the sea.

It was not quite dusk when Huaman set out once more from his home for the center of the city. He had loosened his sandals—he would take them off during his interview with the Inca—and onto his shoulder he had hefted a big rock, his version of the symbolic burden each man in the empire carried when he entered into

Pachacuti's presence. Senior members of the Inca family and important *curacas* and captains carried only a feather on their backs in the Inca's presence, but Huaman had decided to demonstrate in this fashion how seriously he took his obligations to the ruler.

In his hands, Huaman once again carried a gift, a chased bowl of silver decorated with emeralds, that his father had presented to him only this morning, as his own graduation gift. It was the most precious thing Huaman owned, and he wanted the Inca to have it.

"May it bring more luck than the gift of this afternoon," Huaman found himself wishing fervently, his body tensing again as he thought of that brief and bitter encounter in the garden of gold.

Huaman never found out whether it brought any luck, or even whether the Inca liked the precious present he had offered. As he stepped into the antechamber to the audience room, two attendants came forward to meet him. They took his bowl, thanked him in the name of the Inca, and assured him that his gift would find its proper place in the collection of tributes that arrived at the palace. Huaman's heart froze. He knew that an endless river of gifts flowed into Cora Cora palace each day from all over the empire. Pachacuti would never even see his bowl.

Perhaps he could tell the Inca about it when they met, Huaman thought anxiously. Tell Pachacuti what the gift meant and why he wanted the Inca to have it. Huaman recalled Pachacuti's face when the Inca had, himself, pierced Huaman's ear and inserted the golden needle. The face had looked so wise. Pachacuti would understand.

Huaman touched the golden pin in his ear. Yes, he would tell the Inca how much he wanted to serve him in every way he could, and how proud he felt to be his subject and belong to the Kingdom of the Sun.

"I am glad I took the big rock and not a feather," he thought. "The Inca will see it and know what it means."

Did the Inca see? or understand? Huaman never knew. He did not get to look into the sad eyes of Pachacuti, nor see the wise, royal face. The interview took place with a screen between them.

When Huaman had stammered out the devotion that lay in the vessel he had brought, Pachacuti's voice came through the screen, formal and fatigued: "The Inca appreciates the gifts of his subjects."

When Huaman tried, facing that forbidding screen, to tell the Inca how firm was his resolution to serve the empire, the cold, resonant voice filtered through the screen sounding the way voices sound inside a large *huaca*, echoing and empty.

"When subjects, *curacas* and captains cordially obey the king, the kingdom enjoys perfect peace and quiet," the voice said.

It was Pachacuti's famous maxim. Huaman had been taught it in school. It was repeated in public at every *Inti Raimi*. It had been proclaimed throughout the land.

The interview was over.

Huaman left the palace carrying his sandals, the rock still on his back. The Pachacuti maxim was true, of course; no reasonable man could deny it. And he would obey the Inca. But cordially? Would his heart be in it? Would he ever again feel as he had this morning: joyous, light, powerful as a falcon? The rock was heavy on his back, the stones of the pavement cold and hard against his feet. Dusk had fallen. The Square of Joy was dark gray. The golden morning seemed long ago and far away.

XII A CHOSEN WOMAN

Ima Sumac sat in the garden of the House of Chosen Women and watched the moonbeams reflect in the golden grasses at her feet. It was an intriguing play of light, the soft silver of the moon trying to penetrate the sharp gold of the grass, and not really succeeding. The gold was clearly the stronger of the two.

Having established that fact, Ima Sumac looked up at the moon. Full and muted white, it seemed to hover straight above her head.

"How small it is," she thought. "How much smaller than the sun."

She remembered then how this contrast between the two heavenly bodies that filled her life each day had first occurred to her when she was still quite small, just five. She was certain of the time because it was very shortly after she had entered her third age, the one that followed being a babe in arms and a dependent infant. It began at five, ended at nine and was, for a girl, a very important time of life. It was the first period in which she was regarded as a responsible person, no longer completely dependent on her parents. Responsible enough to be given tasks of her own—a whole range of them—and expected to discharge them completely and satisfactorily, like everyone else in the family and the *ayllu.*

Having just turned five, Ima Sumac had been allowed for the first time to participate in the rites at the family *huaca,* the bulky round mound of earth at the back of the compound that contained the house of her own family and the houses of all her uncles and aunts, and married cousins. Grandfather had died a year earlier and had been buried in the *huaca* that held the ancestors of all the families in the compound. Everyone had come out to pay their respects at the anniversary of grandfather's death. They had sacrificed a guinea pig and after the diviner read its entrails and forecast the family's fate for the next year, they had roasted the meat and eaten it with *cancu,* the special ritual bread her mother had baked that morning. Then *chicha* was passed around in a wooden goblet—Ima Sumac remembered that because the beaker was tall and heavy and she did not like the taste of the drink. It was sour and bubbled in her stomach after she had swallowed it. Some of the older men had chewed coca leaves at the end of the festivities, which made them look as if they had gone to sleep with their eyes open.

Ima Sumac recalled how the moon had made their eyes look glassy, how it had made the *chicha* in the goblet look like a mirror, and how it had covered the *huaca* in a silver light so that it looked more like a pile of ore in a mine than a resting place for ancestors. Ima Sumac had also seen her own face reflected in the cup of *chicha* and that night she had realized for the first time that it was different from the faces of most other girls in the village: her eyes were larger, her lashes longer, her mouth fuller and more curved. That night, the moon hovering between the two mountain peaks that overlooked the valley of her village seemed to be watching, watching her with a cold and gleaming eye.

The night was also the first time Ima Sumac heard about Cuzco from someone who had himself been to the golden capital. The diviner had been there the year before to see his bishop and, later that evening, he told Ima Sumac's family about the *huacas* of the royal *ayllu*. He described how each deceased Inca sat in his own palace and was served in death as he had been in life with food and drink, gifts and garments woven by the Virgins of the Sun. Ima Sumac's heart had beaten faster as she listened to the diviner's description of the services rendered the Inca, and it had seemed to race when he spoke of the beautiful work done by the Chosen Women who elected to dedicate their lives to the service and worship of the sun. She had thought that she saw the diviner glance at her when he spoke of these Virgins of the Sun, but perhaps that had just been her imagination, or her wish. One could never be certain of anything seen by the light of the moon. It blurred every outline, unlike the sun, which made every shape sharp and clear.

Seven years passed before anyone raised the subject again in Ima Sumac's presence, although dreams of Cuzco and visions of the Virgins of the Sun had teased and haunted her many times. During those seven years, she had learned a smattering of the arts that the Chosen Women mastered to perfection: to spin and weave; prepare the three kinds of bread, *totan* for every day, *huminta* for special occasions, and *cancu* for religious ceremonies. She had learned how to brew the fermented *chicha* from corn and how to make the distilled *viñapu*. And she learned to gather flowers and herbs that were delivered to the Inca's storehouses for use as medicines or to create fragrances for rituals.

The valley of her village was known for a special herb with a lovely smell, which was sent to regions throughout the empire for ceremonial use on state occasions. Ima Sumac had learned to climb like a vicuña to outcrops of rock high up in the mountains to find under the shadows of the stone the hard little plant with the tiny blossoms that gave off such a beautiful fragrance. Sometimes, when the melting snows of spring had loosened the earth, some of these rocks had begun to slide under her feet and once she had jumped off a sliding rock just in time and rolled down the mountain a very long way. But she had managed to clutch the plants in her fist throughout that dizzying descent, and the *ayllu's* foreman, to whom she handed the herbs the same afternoon, had been very pleased.

Later still, after she had turned nine, she was sometimes sent to mind the llama flocks grazing in the mountains. Everyone in the *ayllu* knew that she was as fleet and sure-footed as the llamas and that, under her care, nothing would happen to the herd.

Ima Sumac had liked those long days as a shepherdess, starting out early in the morning, just after the sun had come up, and watching the sun move from one side of the sky to the other, sending its warm, brilliant glances in her direction. She had tried always to move the llamas to the parts of the mountain that the sun was honoring with its presence. The animals, too, seemed happier with the sun warming their backs and lighting their way to the best, greenest bits of pasture.

The weaving and cooking Ima Sumac had learned at home during those years was quite different, of course, from the fine arts she was learning now. The wool she had spun as a child had been rough and the weaving plain. Food had been the simple *puric* diet of *charqui*, the sun-dried llama meat; *chuño*, the freeze-dried potatoes that were cooked into a gruel flavored with red pepper or a lick of salt to which everyone helped themselves from the white rock that was set in the center of the eating-mat during dinner. Ima Sumac's father had liked the *charqui* best, with some spiced *chuño* on the side. Her mother's favorite dish had been ears of corn roasted over the clay stove with the stone rings on top. Her own preference had been *chupe*, a stew made of oca roots and quinoa leaves. It tasted, she had thought, of the mountainside where she had picked her herbs and flowers and watched the llamas.

Chupe was cooked and served in a bowl of clay that had no decoration but did have a handsome shape. Ima Sumac's family ate with wooden spoons which absorbed the flavor of the stew.

After the spoons had been used for some time, one could lick them and the flavor would still be there. Ima Sumac's tongue curled at the memory. She moved her shoulders in a quick shrug to shake off the thought.

Ima Sumac had been troubled and afraid, afraid of losing her familiar world—the things she knew and the people she loved—when the big day came that changed her life: the day the Inca's inspector selected her to become an *aclla cuna*, a Chosen Woman.

The *curaca* had arrived in the village very early because he had

&ۍ   KINGDOM OF THE SUN

wanted to make his rounds before the families set off for their day's work in the fields. He had visited every compound, every house, and of all the girls that were presented to him as eligible maidens because they had reached their twelfth birthday, he had chosen only one: Ima Sumac.

"The name," he had said, "is apt."

When the servants and guards from the House of Chosen Women arrived some weeks later to escort Ima Sumac to Cuzco, they already had a number of other young women in their care. But she had been the only one to leave from her village. And when they had come to the place where the road dipped low from the valley to the river below, and she had realized that from then on she would no longer be able to see her family standing outside the compound to watch her depart, would no longer be able to see the village itself, a tremor of anxiety had flooded through her. She had never looked back—that would not have been proper—but she had felt lonely, even with all the other girls around her. When she had gazed down at the swirling river, and at the swaying bridge arching it, she had also felt afraid.

Ima Sumac looked at the golden llama in the far corner of the garden and smiled. She had been wrong to be afraid. In the two years she had spent at the House since, she had not once been lonely, and life had been absorbing and beautiful.

The House itself was orderly and silent, not like her home in the *ayllu* where there was always the noise of children and animals. The front of the House was carefully guarded and no one was allowed into the main part unless they had an explicit reason and specific permission from the governor who was responsible for the welfare of the Chosen Women of Cuzco. When someone did secure such permission he was met at the end of the corridor by the senior *mamacuna* and escorted to the garden. There all interviews were held.

The garden of the House was a delight. It was a small version of the famous golden gardens of *Coricancha*, the Temple of the Sun, with the most attractive objects of nature reproduced in gold, the sweat of the sun. There were golden leaves and flowers, golden llamas and birds. Ima Sumac's special delight was a golden replica of that sweet-smelling herb she knew so well from her own childhood forays. She also liked the ears of golden corn, with each kernel perfect forever. At home, corn had gone dry after a while and lost its sheen.

What Ima Sumac loved above all at the House was the stone cubicle that was her room. She had never had a room of her own before. At home, in the village, the family hut was divided at night with hangings of thick llama wool so that her parents, her brothers, and she and her sisters could sleep separately. But the hangings did not keep out sounds and someone was always snoring or coughing or speaking out in their sleep. Here, the stone walls were thick and in her room she had complete privacy.

During the day there were the other girls to meet and get to know—*aclla cuna* from all over the empire—each with a story to tell of her own *ayllu* and with memories to impart of her own life as a child, before she had been chosen. Ima Sumac found that interesting, too.

And there had been so much to learn!

Ima Sumac had, of course, known how to spin before she came.

Her mother had taught her before she was six years old. But there was a big difference between spinning the rough fibers of llama wool and the fine soft curls that had been shorn off a vicuña. Vicuña spinning was more difficult; one had to concentrate more and be more careful; but it felt different, too.

At home, the wooden spindle had been solid in her hand and as she twirled the llama shearings around it, Ima Sumac had felt that she was doing a useful, practical job. In the House of Chosen Women, the spindles were made of silver and almost cradled themselves to the hand. The vicuña shearings were fine and gentle so that running them through her fingertips was a delicate pleasure. Also, Ima Sumac knew that the garment for which she was preparing the wool would be a work of art. It was a lovely feeling.

The weaving was even more rewarding. At home, working the loom had been a simple affair once she had learned the rudiments by watching her mother. Woof and warp in plain wool as it came off the spindle: no patterns, no dyes, no decorations. At the House, everything was complex, elaborate. Ima Sumac had not realized how many different kinds of weaving there were: the plain cloth with a warp face, the warp raised to make a pattern; warp face weaving with a float, to create pattern on pattern; the even more intricate richness of tapestry and brocade; the delicate, airy creations of gauze, lace and voile; the durable, double-woven cloth and twills; the special cloth for special items that called for twining, knotting, looping, coiling and fishnet fabrics. The variety was enormous and Ima Sumac loved the discovery of each one and the slow, steady process of mastering them. There were times when she looked at a particularly elaborate tapestry, or an extraordinarily delicate length of lace she had made on her loom, and it seemed to her almost incredible that this could be the work of her hands.

Even more than weaving cloth, Ima Sumac loved creating decorative effects. The *mamacuna* who taught the Chosen Women the art of coloring had told them that the people of Paracas, on the coast to the south, had been great masters of this art and had worked with two hundred different hues. The Incas thought this was excessive. There was no need for that wide a variety, but there were at least four dozen shades Chosen Women could use in the special garments they made for the Inca, for his own use and to bestow on deserving *curacas* and captains. Ima Sumac had already seen an embroidered tunic she had made being awarded to a *curaca* at the last *Inti Raimi* festival. She had seen how pleased the *curaca* looked when the presentation was made and she had caught a glimpse of him at the festival three days later when he was crossing the Square of Joy wearing his new garment. It had given her a thrill she had not experienced before.

"The pride of accomplishment," the *mamacuna* had explained when Ima Sumac had told her about it. "It is a worthy feeling, but you must be careful not to let it capture you. There are many accomplishments yet to be mastered."

How true that had been. After discovering the various dyes and how they could be prepared and applied, Ima Sumac learned the even subtler skill of *ikat,* tie dyeing in predetermined patterns. Great care was required to prepare the designs and make certain they emerged as a rhythmic, regular pattern. But how satisfying it was when one succeeded! Then the cloth was a little world of its own: alive with color but ordered; varied but complete. *Ikat* was

Ima Sumac's favorite work. At the House, she already had a reputation for her taste and skill at it.

Other decorative arts were taught the Chosen Women: embroidery, featherwork, making a garment glitter by applying to it discs and plates of metal. All three produced handsome effects. Ima Sumac discovered, however, that they required a dexterity of hand that she did not possess and a patience that did not come to her naturally. She could do creditable work but she did not enjoy it as she did the *ikat*, and there were other girls at the House who were better at each one of them than Ima Sumac was.

"We all serve the Inca and the sun in our own way," the *mamacuna* had said.

There was one art in which Ima Sumac wished she could excel but knew she could not. That was the art of painting cloth: sizing the material so that it became stiff and then using a brush and a heavy, creamy dye to make the cloth come alive: not only with patterns like the ones she could create with *ikat*, but with animals and even with figures of people. One girl at the House was particularly good at this and her last creation, a stole, had gone to the Inca's chief wife.

Another new range of knowledge had opened up for Ima Sumac in the preparation of food and beverages. The diet Ima Sumac and her family had adhered to at home had been simple and repetitive. At the House, she was taught to prepare food for the Inca, for the high priest and his bishops, and for special state and ritual occasions. She had learned to prepare dishes she had never even heard of before: wild duck and partridge from the highlands; frogs and snails from faraway lakes; mushrooms, pineapples, papaya, blackberries, strawberries and raspberries from the other side of the mountains; and from the sea, where the empire ended, fish, and small, extremely tasty creatures that also lived in the water. Every-one of these dishes had its own intricacies in the way it was cleaned, cooked, spiced, and arranged for serving.

The beverages, too, were richer and more varied than anything Ima Sumac had known. At home, they had drunk water, or *chicha* on special occasions. At the House, Ima Sumac had learned about fruit juices of all kinds, had discovered the rich, sweet drink that came from the other side of the mountain called chocolate, and had learned to make many kinds of *chicha*, with varying degrees of refinement and fermentation. The most delicate, the most highly refined, was kept for the ceremonies at the Temple of the Sun.

Preparing a cup of *chicha* for a sunrise service—the high priest had sent one of his best golden beakers for it—was the closest Ima Sumac had come as yet to rendering personal service to the sun itself. Whenever she thought of it, a wave of awe and wonder washed over her that left her trembling. Perhaps, she thought, that was because she had not yet learned the most precious knowledge the House of Chosen Women could teach: the tending of the shrines of the sun. Ima Sumac knew that this was a task to be approached with concentration and delicacy, more, much more, than the delicacy and concentration needed for *ikat*. Tending a shrine required that one be completely pure in body, mind and spirit, so that one's whole being was fused together to feel like a flame, like a ray of the sun. The divine star deserved no less than that.

Tending a shrine, Ima Sumac had already been told, required a

Chosen Woman to fast before she approached the sanctuary and learn special movements and dances. It demanded that she keep the cloth in the temple immaculate and the altars, vessels and images burnished. Most important, it charged her with tending the eternal fire that the high priest himself received each year from the sun. That fire demonstrated to the people of the world that the sun was with them always, and it made clear to the nations of the empire that the warmth and nourishment the sun gave them could be secured best by obeying the Inca, the sun's own son.

Ima Sumac had not yet been initiated into the mysteries of serving the sun. These mysteries were taught in the third, the last year at the House, after each girl had made her decision about the future: whether she wanted to return to her family; put herself and her skills at the disposition of the Inca, to choose for her a way of life he considered best for the empire; or dedicate herself to the service of the sun. Ima Sumac had not yet made that final choice.

She had been offered a glimpse of what it would be like to serve the Inca. The *mamacuna* who taught her *ikat* had taken her to the palace just before the *Inti Raimi* festival to deliver to the queen a patterned tunic Ima Sumac had completed the week before. She had mixed a pale yellow and a very soft red, creating an effect that reminded her of the color of a mountaintop when the sun just began to climb over its peak. The pattern had been one of open triangles ascending, which looked like the first rays of the sun sparking off the snow on the summit. The queen had liked the cloth so well she had given it to her oldest daughter and had instructed the daughter to take Ima Sumac and the *mamacuna* through the women's section of the palace.

It had been very luxurious. The doorways were covered with hangings of vicuña or feathers, worked very airily, so that the light could filter through. The floors were covered with the skins of animals, so that walking about the room felt soft and warm underfoot. Niches in the palace walls held handsome objects: bowls and vases of clay, painted all over; or goblets and plates of gold, with hammered and engraved designs. The ladies of the palace sat on stools covered with vicuña cloth and slept on sheets of vicuña, covering themselves with vicuña blankets. They wore ankle-length tunics rich with embroidery or featherwork; their shawls were works of art and they changed them each day. And the pins that held the shawls together below the throat were of gold or silver, with heads molded to look like fans, flower petals, or even the round disc of the sun.

The ladies of the palace had a great many servants, whose work they supervised, but they did no work themselves. They seemed busy, however, and they certainly looked sumptuous and noble.

On the way home from the palace, the *mamacuna* had said: "The queen seemed pleased with you."

Ima Sumac knew what this meant. It implied that if she chose to serve the Inca and the empire, she might find herself in the royal palace as one of the Inca's many secondary wives, or as a consort to one of the young princes. If she chose this kind of life, the Inca might also decide to award her to one of the *curacas*, or to one of the military officers, for special merit. There was really no telling just where she would be making her life, or with whom, if she took that road. It would certainly be an existence of comfort and importance. As wife or consort of an Inca, *curaca* or captain, she would be treated with respect and deference as long as she lived.

And yet . . .

After the visit to the palace, Ima Sumac had spent several nights as she was doing now, sitting in the garden of the House of Chosen Women, among the golden grasses and animals, thinking about it all. It would be a good life and a worthy one, she had thought, putting herself at the disposition of the Inca, with many rewards and compensations. But there was something about it she did not like. It made her feel a little soiled, the way she had felt when she was small and had come back from a day of searching for herbs and flowers: content with a good day's work but spotted all over, with clumps of dirt clinging to her legs and arms, sticking to the soles of her feet and settling between her toes and under her fingernails. Her first impulse then had always been to go to the river and wash. But she could not go to the river and wash off the feeling inside her at the thought of being awarded by the Inca, as a special mark of his favor, to some man, however noble and worthy. The Inca did the same with lands and llamas, with chased vessels of gold and silver and, yes, even with some of the special garments they wove here at the House of Chosen Women. She herself made, or helped to make, these garments that were given away— much as she herself would be given away. There was something unfitting about that. It could not be wrong, since the Inca himself did it and it was the custom in the empire. Ima Sumac knew that many of the girls in the House liked the idea of being chosen and awarded as a special mark of the Inca's favor and living the life of luxury that went with this state. But she found it difficult to think of herself as a possession, to be given away like a tunic, a belt, or a *chuspa*.

Still, to grace and run the palace of a young man like the prince who had come to the House today did seem exciting. There was something about that prince Ima Sumac had liked very much, from the instant she set eyes on him. There was a leanness about him, a verve and an inner fire that made her think of the tales she had heard in the compound at home of the wild puma that sometimes appeared in the highlands.

Huaman was his name: falcon. Yes, that was a good name for him. There was a soaring quality to him in addition to the wildness, and that gleam she had seen in the young prince's eye was like the glitter in a falcon's eye when it spread its wings and took off for the sky. She had often seen falcons do just that when she was minding the llamas. She had always made certain then there were no baby animals within the bird's reach.

Huaman lived in Cuzco now, Ima Sumac had been told, but if she became his wife she would go with him to his own city, Chan-Chan, when his father died and he took over the rule of the kingdom. Their children, of course, would be reared in Cuzco, at least the oldest. But she would be living in that city by the water, where houses were painted inside and gardens were not made of gold and permanent like her garden here, but had grasses and flowers that blossomed and withered.

Ima Sumac was not at all certain she would like that. Still, the Chimú were a worthy people. She had heard about them. They were valiant and they had many accomplishments to their credit. Chan-Chan was not just another small *ayllu*. It was a big city. Not, of course, as big and glorious as Cuzco, the navel of the world, but estimable in its own way. The Chimú, she had heard, had built roads in their kingdom even before they joined the empire, and had learned how to bring water to their dry lands. They even had a fertilizer of their own to help the crops grow, derived not from human beings or llamas but from birds, birds who lived on clumps of land in the water, beyond the edge of the world. Ima Sumac found that idea hard to grasp. How could anyone or anything live beyond the edge of the world? Still, she had been told that these birds did that, and so did the fish and the little water creatures she had learned to prepare for the Inca's table. All these were drawn out of the sea with nets by special men who traveled beyond the edge of the world in boats. It was all very strange.

Ima Sumac knew that the Inca Pachacuti valued and honored the Chimú and that, before they became part of the empire, they had had a large kingdom of their own. They still ruled that kingdom, as vassals of the Sapa Inca.

This was as it should be, Ima Sumac thought. Whatever the Chimú might know, the Incas certainly knew better, and whatever the Chimú's achievements, they could only be pale copies of the accomplishments of her own people who, as children of the sun, brought completion and perfection to the lives and worlds of all others.

She herself could help to do that! Bring Inca perfection to people who still languished without it.

The idea made Ima Sumac sit up very straight on her stool in the golden garden. She was aware that in all the new lands that joined the empire, the Inca immediately ordered the establishment of a Temple of the Sun, and a House of Chosen Women to tend the temple.

She could ask to be sent to one of these Houses in the new lands, where she could serve in the temple and have a share in showing other peoples the glory and satisfaction of belonging to the Kingdom of the Sun. That would be a very exciting thing to do. Perhaps they would send her to Chan-Chan? She knew that a Temple of the Sun and a House of Chosen Women had been built there shortly after the Chimú joined the realm.

There had, in fact, been some trouble about that, she recalled. The Chimú had claimed that they had their own laws and deities and did not need any new ones. Their laws had served the kingdom well enough, they had argued, and their gods had nourished them and guided them to power and to glory. The Inca Pachacuti had been very patient with the Chimú. He had pointed out that while their laws had served to prevent chaos, Inca laws established a permanent order. Since everybody in the Inca empire knew his task and his place, his duties and rewards, his obligations and privileges, no one had any reason to rebel. They were all secure. They knew that they could depend on their families, their *ayllu*, their *curacas* and, finally, on the Inca and, through his intercession, the sun itself. Clearly, there could be nothing better, or equal to, being part of such a perfect scheme.

Many of the Chimú lords had thought this true as soon as they heard about Inca ways. But it took several years, and many battles with the Inca army, to convince the king.

He was convinced in the end, Ima Sumac had heard, by Pachacuti himself, who honored the Chimú king by letting him walk in procession with princes of the blood during the *Inti Raimi* festival in the year that followed the Chimú's adherence to the realm.

The matter of the gods had been even more difficult, Ima Sumac recalled. The Chimú claimed that their own gods, the fox who represented wisdom and, above all, the sea which nourished them, deserved their worship. Pachacuti had said that they could continue to worship these gods but that they must acknowledge as superior to them—since it shone over them all—the sun. That was the time the big blasphemy had been uttered in Chan-Chan and there had been consternation in Cuzco. The Chimú, it seemed, had said that the sun did not serve them well. In the summer it beat down on their bodies, dried their lands and withered their gardens. If they were to worship any star in the skies they would prefer the moon, whose light was soft and gentle and did not cause flowers to shrivel or make men and women heavy and drowsy with fatigue.

The Inca Pachacuti had finally set the Chimú right on this superstition. He had pointed out that the moon was the wife of the sun and could thus be honored with devotion. But it was the sun that gave the light, warmth and nourishment that men—all men everywhere—lived by: men, their animals, and their plants.

And so the Chimú had built a Temple of the Sun, bigger and more splendid than their own old shrines. Inca priests performed the rituals and the inhabitants of the House of Chosen Women nearby provided the care and services the temple required. Many of the Chimú now came to worship in the temple, but there were also still large numbers who went to the old sanctuaries and paid homage to the fox, to the sea, to the moon, and to some little wooden idol they kept in a special shrine.

The young prince from Chan-Chan, Ima Sumac reflected, although very attractive, had that strange air about him of people who do not concentrate their devotion on one deity, who worship whatever appeals to them because it has at some time, in some way, lit up their lives. This young prince of Chan-Chan, for example, was evidently moon-struck. The tone of his voice, the light in his eyes when he had presented her with that black jar and talked to her about the moon was filled with a passion and devotion that was due only to the sun. And he had been educated at the academy! Not only that, but the *mamacuna* had told her that he had distinguished himself at the graduation exercises, had given almost as good an account of himself as the Inca's own son.

It was very confusing. Ima Sumac sighed, then turned with a start as she heard steps behind her. It was her favorite *mamacuna*, the one who had taken her to the palace with her piece of *ikat*, and had been present today during the interview with the prince.

"It is late to be alone in the garden," the *mamacuna* said. "Morning will soon be here."

Ima Sumac, reminded of time and place, shivered. The cold of the hour before dawn was in the air. If the grass under her feet had been green, it would now have begun to gather tiny drops of water.

"I am troubled, *mamacuna*," Ima Sumac said.

The *mamacuna* nodded. "I know. The time for choice has come. It is not easy. But you have seen enough of what each choice holds."

Suddenly, Ima Sumac realized that the past few weeks, the visit to the palace, the encounter with the prince, had been tests, deliberately designed by the *mamacuna* to help Ima Sumac discover where her true vocation lay.

Memories and feelings, from the night she had first heard about Cuzco to this afternoon's meeting, tumbled through her head in rapid succession until, all at once, everything fell into place, clearly and sharply, as if lit up by the sun itself.

Her mind, which had whirled about before, seemed to stand still in a ray of recognition. Despite the cold and the darkness, she felt warm and at peace. Her eyes met those of the *mamacuna*.

No words were exchanged, but slowly, gravely, the *mamacuna* inclined her head.

Ima Sumac knew. She would not go home to her village when her three years of study at the House were completed. The time of gathering herbs and flowers, and taking care of the llama herds, was over. Village life as a grown woman, while warm and secure, held no charms for her. She would have to marry a boy from the village, help him in the fields, look after the house, bear children and rear them, and never again feel fine vicuña under her fingers, spend the day mixing dyes or designing a pattern of *ikat*. If she went back to her village, she would never again see the sun dance on the walls of *Coricancha*, the sun's own temple, or watch the sun play on the roofs of Cuzco, its very own city.

Ima Sumac knew as well that she did not want to become a Chosen Woman at the disposition of the Inca and the empire. It was a comfortable and interesting life, but not what her heart desired.

And marrying the prince of Chan-Chan?

That would be an adventure, she thought, a life of challenge and excitement. It appealed to her greatly. But if challenge was what she wanted, she told herself, she could find it without tying herself to a moonstruck young man whose actions and reactions one could never be sure of. She could become a *mitmakona,* a Chosen Woman who served in a House set down among alien people who had to be taught the ways of the Inca and the virtues of worshiping the sun.

"But," Ima Sumac decided, "there is one kind of life more exciting still. And this will be my choice. My final choice."

Sitting in the garden under the moonlight, which had become almost ghostly pale as dawn came close, Ima Sumac resolved that she would become a Virgin of the Sun.

She would spend the next year delving deeply into the secrets of serving the sun and thereafter dedicate her life to that service. She knew this meant a commitment that was total and permanent. Having pledged herself to the sun's service, she would never leave the House of Chosen Women again for any personal reason: not to see her family; not to see a man to whom she was close and who was close to her; not to share in the tasks and celebrations of an *ayllu,* any *ayllu.*

Instead, she would dance the grave, solemn steps of the Virgins of the Sun during the *Inti Raimi,* barefoot and dressed in white. Once each year, she would go to *Coricancha* to renew her vows, accompanied always by a *mamacuna,* by servants and guards with their weapons at ready. The rest of the time, she would tend the temple, the golden temple here in Cuzco. She would make fine garments for its priests; prepare food for its sacrifices; and, above all, play her part, however infinitesimal, in watching over the holy fire by which the world lived.

PART THREE

XIII TRACKING THE INCA

1. IN THEIR HOMELAND:

Machu Picchu. The most impressive Inca site is Machu Picchu, reputedly the refuge of the last of the Incas. Machu Picchu has remains of every structure that was characteristic of Inca life and institutions: a Temple of the Sun, and a "hitching post of the sun"; a House of Chosen Women, palaces, fountains, a *huaca* for the dead, well-preserved agricultural terraces on the mountain sides that ring the ruins.

Machu Picchu means "Old Peak." The ruins were discovered by the American explorer-politician Hiram Bingham, early in the twentieth century. In an exciting account of the discovery of Machu Picchu, Bingham writes:

"The sanctuary was lost for centuries because this ridge (on which Machu Picchu is situated) is in the most inaccessible corner of the most inaccessible section of the central Andes. No part of the highlands

KINGDOM OF THE SUN

of Peru is better defended by natural bulwarks—a stupendous canyon whose rock is granite, and whose precipices are frequently a thousand feet sheer, presenting difficulties which daunt the most ambitious modern mountain climbers. Yet, here, in a remote part of the canyon, on this narrow ridge flanked by tremendous precipices, a highly civilized people, artistic, inventive, well organized, and capable of sustained endeavor, at some time in the distant past built themselves a sanctuary for the worship of the sun."

It is still not easy to reach Machu Picchu. It takes a plane trip to Lima, another plane trip from there to Cuzco, a half day's ride through the Sacred Valley of the Incas on the railway that negotiates a very precipitous climb with the aid of considerable "back-switching." Finally, it takes a trip by bus, or horse, up the serpentine road that leads to the top of an Andean peak and the amazing site of Machu Picchu.

Cuzco. "Cuzco, the golden" is golden no more. The conquistadors stripped it of everything that glittered, except the sun-drenched sky and pellucid air that still lend sparkle to the city. The rest of it tends to be gray but much of that gray is massive rock and the carefully worked stones of Inca days which can still be seen throughout Cuzco. They look exactly as they did in Inca days in the gigantic fortress of Sacsahuaman that overlooks the city, and in the baths of the Inca not far from the fortress. They exist within the town in walls and in the foundations of innumerable buildings.

Coricancha, for example, the famous Temple of the Sun, was used by the Spaniards as the foundation for a monastery and today houses a Dominican convent. The original temple structure, with its rooms for sun and moon, thunder and lightning, and the rainbow, can still be traced. Throughout the city, one can still see the trapezoid doorways and niches characteristic of Inca architecture.

The town common that used to be golden Cuzco's "Square of Joy," is now the *Plaza de Armas*, but it is still the focal point of the city and is used for celebrations, both Inca and Spanish.

Puruchucu. Not far from Lima, this is the restored residence of an Inca *curaca* who governed the important province of Rimac. Beautifully and accurately restored, the residence shows reception rooms and bedrooms, storage chambers and a terrace dedicated to the worship of the sun. The restoration is complete up to and including a kitchen and pantry, displaying the food this *curaca* and his family ate, and indicating how it was prepared.

Pachacamac. This site, too, is not far from Lima and is partially restored. It contains the ruins of the Temple of the Sun that was built on Inca orders at the edge of the sea, as well as the ruins of the famous oracle of Rimac, which was to the people of the Inca empire what Delphi was to the Greeks. The site, in a small but excellent museum, displays details of daily life in the Kingdom of the Sun such as costumes, domestic utensils, agricultural implements, weapons and an array of working tools for both men and women. It also has a completely restored House of Chosen Women.

Cajamarca. The site of the historic encounter between the Inca and the conquistadors is now an almost completely Spanish town in the colonial style. But it still contains, unaltered, the building in which Atahuallpa was imprisoned and the stone chamber that was filled with gold for his ransom. Also extant is the town square in which Atahuallpa, after his ransom was paid, was executed.

Pisac. Many villages dot the Andean highlands where descendants of the Inca live much as they did in the days of the empire, although less securely and less well. One of the most illustrative is Pisac, not far from Cuzco.

In Pisac, Inca town elders run the community as if they were *curacas,* and the town market, held once a week, has men and women squatting on the ground with their piles of peppers or potatoes, herbs or spices piled up on mats in front of them. Much of the trade is barter, carried on in silence.

Nueva Esperanza. This is one of the "new towns" that have sprung up around Lima, established and administered on much the same principles that governed an *ayllu* during the days of the Inca Empire. Television antennae already spike some of the huts but the community spirit is strong and the language spoken is Quechua, the tongue that unified the Inca realm.

Nueva Esperanza is a fascinating example of the strongest and most serviceable traits of Inca social organization that have survived and of the way these traits can be blended into modern life.

2. THROUGH SITES OF THE GREAT PRECURSORS:

Chavín de Huántar. This site of the earliest of the precursor civilizations is hard to get to. You take off from a beautiful valley nestled between the black and white cordilleras called the *Callejon de Huaylas,* where devastating earthquakes and landslides occur with tragic frequency.

A very bad road leads from the *Callejon* up the white cordillera and takes you to a surprisingly well preserved temple complex encompassing some thousand square feet. There are plazas and terraces, sunken courts, raised platforms and stone structures facing the cardinal points of the compass. And there is a castle, three stories high, with a maze of galleries, rooms, stairs, ramps and—the greatest puzzle of all—ventilating shafts. What makes this complex architectural and engineering sophistication so astonishing is that it is at least twenty-five hundred years old.

Paracas. A peninsula about a hundred fifty miles south of Lima, tawny desert except where irrigation has created strips and spots of green, is the heart of the Paracas civilization, world-renowned for its textiles. You can see some of those textiles, and how they were made, in the museum of Paracas, which displays such implements as cactus needles and scissors made of shell, balls of cotton shading from cream to chocolate-colored, sewing baskets woven of rush and paintbrushes made of human hair.

Nazca. Not far from Paracas is the famous valley in which the Nazca laid out their astronomical design. The design can still be seen just as the Nazca left it, but to get the full impact it has to be seen from the air, with the plane flying low and slowly.

Tiahuanaco. One has to leave Peru and cross Lake Titicaca to the Bolivian side to see the great remains of the Tiahuanaco civilization, with their famous masterpiece "the gateway of the sun," which the Inca maintained was God's "sampler" for the creation of the world.

Chan-Chan. North of Lima, on the coast, Chan-Chan is easy to reach. And what remains of it is fascinating. There are outlines of houses, streets, reservoirs, storage rooms, and the famous sunken gardens. Also extant are the evocative remains of a court of council, with a throne at one end—the end facing the sea—and large stone niches for the litters of attending lords. Nearby is what today's Peruvians call *"El Dragon,"* the ruins of a Chimú temple. It has the sculpted outer walls which, along with painted inner walls, graced the cities of the Chimú and made them attractive and gay.

3. IN THE MUSEUMS OF PERU, THE UNITED STATES AND EUROPE:
The most magnificent collections of Inca civilization, and the civilizations of the Incas' famous precursors, are, naturally, to be found in Peru. The best are:
The National Museum of Anthropology and Archeology in Lima offers a full and fascinating array of objects from the lives of the Incas and their predecessors. Represented are architecture and art, ceramics, metal work, and textiles. In a tall glass case in the heart of the museum, stands the magnificent "man in the mantle," an Inca wearing a floor-length tunic, which displays to perfection the skill of the weaver-artists of Paracas.

The Rafael Larco Herrera Museum, also in Lima, has a notable collection of pottery, particularly of the Moche, which is so realistic that it tells a great deal about the way people lived and worked, about their pleasures and pains. The museum also has beautiful samples of the glazed black pottery of the Chimú, with its moon-silver sheen.

The Mujica Gallo Museum, also in Lima, has the world's greatest collection of gold objects from Inca times. Seeing these golden masks and earrings, scepters, goblets and plates makes one understand why the Spaniards thought they had finally found *El Dorado* when they came to the land of the Inca.

Museums in the United States with small but handsome collections representing the Inca and their precursors include:
   The Metropolitan Museum of Art in New York;
   The Museum of Primitive Art in New York;
   The American Museum of Natural History in New York;
   The Textile Museum in Washington, D.C.;
   The Art Institute of Chicago;
   The Peabody Museum of Harvard University;
   The University Museum of the University of Pennsylvania.

In Europe, the most interesting collections of Inca objects are in:
   The British Museum in London;
   The Museum für Völkerkunde in Berlin;
   The Museum für Völkerkunde in Munich;
   The Musée de l'Homme in Paris;
   The Museum of Ethnography in Göteborg, Sweden.

4. IN WRITTEN RECORDS:

Since the Inca had no written language, no original documentary sources exist from the days of the empire. The closest we can come to authentic accounts of life in the Kingdom of the Sun are the records left by two men, both of part-Inca parentage, whose descriptions date from the generation immediately following the conquest. One of them was a writer, the other primarily an illustrator.

The writer is Garcilaso de la Vega, who calls his fascinating, if not always totally dependable, volume *The Royal Commentaries of the Inca*. There is an English translation, edited by Alain Gheerbrant, and published in paperback by Avon Books, New York.

The illustrator is Poma de Ayala, whose original drawings are at the Ethnological Institute in Paris, but have been widely reproduced.

A book that contains many of Poma de Ayala's drawings is *Realm of the Incas* by Victor W. von Hagen. The book exists in paperback, published by The New American Library, New York.

Garcilaso de la Vega and Poma de Ayala offer accounts with an essentially pro-Inca viewpoint. Describing Inca life from the other end of the spectrum, the conquistador Sarmiento de Gamboa gives his version of the Inca realm, which is as jaundiced as Garcilaso's is rosy. Sarmiento de Gamboa's report has been translated into English by a great British Incaist, Sir Clements R. Markham, under the title *History of the Incas*. It is published by the Hakluyt Society in Cambridge, England.

Three other conquistadors wrote accounts of Inca society as they encountered it. Their prejudices and preconceptions are evident, but their reports fascinating all the same. The three are:

Pedro Sancho, by his own description "secretary to Francisco Pizarro, and Scrivener to his Army." Pedro Sancho titled his work *An Account of the Conquest of Peru*. It has been translated into English by a famous American Peruvianist, Philip Ainsworth Means, and is published by the Cortes Society, New York.

Pedro Pizarro, brother to Francisco, wrote an account he called *Relation and Conquest of the Kingdoms of Peru*. That, also, has been translated by Philip Ainsworth Means, and is published by the Cortes Society, New York.

Capt. Baltasar de Ocampo published, in 1610, his *Account of the Province of Vilcapampa and a Narrative of the Execution of the Inca Tupac Amaru*. The work is considered one of the more dependable accounts of Inca life, as it survived one generation after the conquest, and of the execution of Tupac Amaru I. It was published, in English translation, by the Hakluyt Society, Cambridge, England.

A good and concise description of Inca life, and the most colorful account of the historic encounter between the Incas and the Spaniards, was written in the nineteenth century by an American historian, William H. Prescott. It is called *The Conquest of Peru* and is published in paperback by The New American Library, New York.

The search for, and discovery of, Machu Picchu is recounted in fascinating detail by the explorer who found the famous site, Hiram Bingham. His book is called *Lost City of the Incas: The Story of Machu Picchu and Its Builders* and has been published in paperback by Atheneum, New York.

The great precursor civilizations of the Inca are described concisely, but perhaps too technically for the general reader, by another noted American Peruvianist, J. Alden Mason. His book, *The Ancient Civilizations of Peru* is published in paperback by Penguin Books, an English publisher with United States headquarters in Baltimore, Maryland.

GLOSSARY

A Note on Pronunciation
a is pronounced ah, as in *a*rt
e is pronounced ay, as in *e*nd
i is pronounced ee, as in *is*
o is pronounced oh, as in p*o*t
u is pronounced oo, as in b*u*ll
x is pronounced sh, as in *sh*adow
j is pronounced h', as in the Scottish lo*ch*
ch is pronounced as in *ch*ildren, not as in choral
c is pronounced k, as in *k*ing, at the beginning of a word
   but becomes s, as in *s*entence, in the middle of a word
qu is pronounced k, as in *k*ing
hu is pronounced w, as in *w*ater.
All vowels are pronounced separately, as in ch*a*os.

ACCLA CUNA—A "Chosen Woman"; the elite of the Incas' young women, selected each year to become either wives of the Inca and high nobility or priestesses called "Virgins of the Sun."

AMAUTA—A teacher-historian-philosopher who instructed young princes in their academy in Cuzco.

AWKI—A young prince before he graduated from the academy and underwent the initiation ceremonies which made him an INCA.

AYLLU—The core community of the Incas; the equivalent of a village or a neighborhood.

AYMARA—A highland tribe that was, at one point, neighbor and rival to the Inca. The tribe's language survives and is also called Aymara.

BOLA—A sling loaded with a fist-sized rock, which constituted one of the weapons in the Inca arsenal.

BORLA—The tasselled headband worn by the Inca, equivalent to a crown.

CANCU—A special bread baked for ritual purposes only.

CAPAC INTI RAIMI—The words mean "King Sun Festival." It was the annual celebration of the summer solstice, the most important festival in the Inca calendar.

CHACU—The word means "stop." It is the designation for the annual hunt organized by the Inca.

CHASQUI—An official Inca runner who relayed messages.

CHARQUI—Dried meat.

CHICHA—A fermented drink brewed by the Inca, equivalent to beer or wine.

CHUÑO—A spiced potato gruel.

CHUPE—A vegetable stew.

COCA—A dried leaf with tranquilizing and energy-releasing properties. The Inca used it for ritual purposes.

COLLA—The upper reaches of the highlands, with an elevation of 12,000 feet or more.

CORDILLERA—The high mountain range that runs throughout the Western hemisphere, from the Rockies to the tip of South America.

CORICANCHA—The words mean "The Place of Gold." It was the main temple of the Inca Empire, located in the capital of Cuzco.

COSCO—The word means "navel" and is the root of Cuzco, the Inca capital. The Inca thought of their capital as "the navel of the world."

CURACA—A high Inca official.

GUANO—A fertilizer made of bird droppings. The ownership and distribution of *guano* was in the days of the Inca—and is today—a government monopoly.

HAUCAIPATE—The word means "the square of joy." It was the name of Cuzco's central plaza under the Inca, renamed by the Spaniards *plaza de armas*, the square of arms.

HAYLLI, HAYLLI—An exclamation uttered by spectators during a race or other competitive event. The literal equivalent would be "hail, hail"; the meaning is something like "go man, go."

HUMINTA—A special bread baked for Inca festivals.

ICHU—A hard highland grass.

IKAT—The Inca skill of the tie dyeing in predetermined patterns.

INCA—The word describes the tribe, the people, and their ruler.

LLAUTU—A royal headdress.

MACANA—A two-edged sword.

MAMACUNA—A woman teacher and supervisor of "Chosen Women."

MAMANIC—The word means "our mother." It is the affectionate term Inca subjects used for their queen.

MAYOC—Supervisor.

MITA—A tax, paid with labor.

MITIMA—The Inca colonizing system.

MITMAKONA—Colonists.

MONTAÑA—The word means "the mountainous region" in Spanish. In Peru, it is used to describe the hills and valleys on the Eastern slopes of the Andes.

NYOSTA—Unmarried girl of the Inca royal family.

OREJONES—A Spanish word, meaning "big ears." It was the appellation the Spaniards used for Inca nobles whose earlobes were distended by the heavy ear ornaments they wore.

PACHACA CURACA—A supervisor in charge of 100 *purics*.

PALYA—A married woman of the Inca royal family.

PAX INCAICA—The words are Latin, meaning "Inca Peace." It describes the concept the Inca had of a peaceful realm administered by them.

Pica Conka Kamayok—A supervisor in charge of 50 *purics*.

Pica Curaca—A supervisor in charge of 5,000 *purics*.

Pirca—A paving composite, made of clay, pebbles, and maize leaves.

Pirua—A royal storage house. Such warehouses were scattered throughout the empire.

Puric—The individual Inca male citizen.

Quechua—The language of the Inca, which also became the language of the Inca empire and is still spoken today.

Quipu—A memory device used by the Inca, who had no written language. It was used mainly for numerical messages and is a kind of abacus on strings.

Quipucamayu—A person who has mastered the manipulation of the *quipu*; the Inca equivalent of a mathematician.

Santiago—Spanish for St. James. Santiago was the conquistadors' patron saint.

Sapa—The word is Inca and means "wise one." It is a title, equivalent to the English "sir."

Sinchi—A tribal leader.

Tambo—An inn. The word is still used in Peru today. It derives from *tampu*.

Tampu—The Inca word for the government-administered hostelries that dotted the empire.

Tokoyrikoq—An Inca inspector.

Totan—The Incas' daily bread.

Tupamaros—Political revolutionaries in South America. The word is a contraction of Tupac Amaru, an Inca who was beheaded by the conquistadors and whose descendant fought the Spaniards two centuries after the conquest.

Viñapa—A distilled liquor used by the Inca mainly for ceremonial occasions. The equivalent of brandy.

Waranca Curaca—Supervisor of 1,000 *purics*.

Yachahuasi—The academy for Inca princes.

Important Place Names

APURIMAC—A river in Peru, spanned by an Inca suspension bridge.

CAJAMARCA—A town of the Inca empire, where the conquistadors first met the ruling Inca, Atahuallpa, whom they later imprisoned in Cajamarca. The town still exists.

CALLEJON DE HUAYLAS—A beautiful highland valley in Peru, particularly vulnerable to earthquakes and floods.

CHAN CHAN—The capital of the Chimú civilization on the Pacific coast of Peru, north of Lima. The ruins of Chan Chan still exist.

CHAVÍN DE HUANTÁR—An archeological site of the Chavín civilization, just east of the *Callejon de Huaylas.*

CORA CORA—The original palace of the Inca rulers. Its walls can still be seen in Cuzco.

CUZCO—The capital of the Inca empire and an important city of Peru.

EL DORADO—The Spanish words mean "The Golden One." It was the conquistadors' vision of a mythical kingdom rich in gold. For a time they thought that Cuzco was the place.

MACHU PICCHU—Magnificent Inca ruins, high up in the Andes north of Cuzco, generally thought to be the last refuge of the Inca royal family after the conquest.

MAULE—A river which constituted the southernmost frontier of the Inca empire. Today, it marks the Peruvian border of Chile.

NAZCA—A Pacific coastal region, south of Lima; the heartland of the Nazca civilization.

PARACAS—A peninsula on the Pacific coast, south of Lima; the heartland of the Paracas civilization.

PARAMONGA—A city off the Pacific coast north east of Lima, with a fortress built by the Chimú.

PACHACAMAC—Ruins of a sanctuary and palace, just south of Lima, dating to pre-Inca days.

PISAC—A highland village not far from Cuzco, where many Inca customs survive.

PURUCHUCU—The reconstituted residence of an Inca governor, east of Lima.

QUITO—Once part of the Inca Empire, now the capital of Ecuador.

RIMAC—Ruins of an old sanctuary near Lima. In both Inca and pre-Inca days this sanctuary was known for its oracle—an equivalent to the Delphi of the Greeks.

SACSAHUAMAN—A massive fortress outside Cuzco, where the Inca fought the conquistadors in the final battle for the Inca capital.

TIAHUANÁCO—Magnificent ruins, on the Bolivian side of Lake Titicaca, of the powerful civilization of the Tiahuanáco.

TITICACA—A large lake high up in the Andes, constituting today the border between Peru and Bolivia.

TUCUMÁN—A city in Argentina that constituted the easternmost outpost of the Inca empire.

TUMBES—A port city in northern Peru, where the conquistadors landed.

INDEX

Spaniards, 26, 76, 101, 133
  accounts of Inca life, 93, 241–42
  destruction of Inca empire, 4–7, 15,
    154–67, 176, 235
  rebellion against, 177
statistical methods, 131. *See also*
  government, record-keeping;
  quipu
storehouse network, 10, 65, 110–11,
  124, 239
sun-father, 16, 18–20, 65, 79

Tale of the Shining Mantle, 20
taxes. *See* mita
Temples of the Sun, 147, 234
  Coricancha, 76, 81–83, 104, 163–
    64, 236
textiles, 57, 69, 147–49, 239
  of Paracas, 47–48, 147–48, 168,
    238–39
Tiahuanaco, 22–23, 51–55, 239
Titicaca, Lake, 16, 19, 52–55, 161

tokoyrikoq ("see-alls"). *See* inspection network
Topa Inca Yupanqui (tenth Inca), 21,
  33–34
trade, 39, 64–65, 174, 237
trepanning, 153
Tupac Amaru I (thirteenth Inca),
  176–77, 242
Tupac Amaru II, 176
Tupamaros, 177

Viracocha (creator of universe). *See*
  Pachacuti
Viracocha (eighth Inca), 30–33
Virgins of the Sun, 69, 91, 93, 98, 101
von Hagen, Victor, 125, 141, 241

weaving. *See* textiles
welfare state, 4, 8–10, 32, 68

Yahuar Huacac (seventh Inca), 29–30,
  52

985   KAR   352-77

Karen

KINGDOM OF THE SUN

DATE DUE

MY 31 7			
SE 23 77			
DE 23 77			
OCT 3 78			
APR 21 80			
NO 2 '8			
NO 4 '83			
APR			
APR 1 6 1985			
MY 16 '85			
SEP 20 '8			
AP 23 '90